Release Density & Shift Your Life

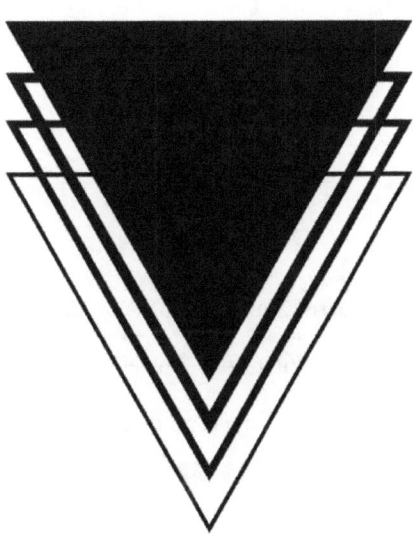

An Interactive Guidebook by
Arielle Sterling

ARIELLE STERLING

Release Density & Shift Your Life

An Interactive Guidebook

By Arielle Sterling

Copyright © 2017 Arielle Sterling

All rights reserved.

No part of this guidebook may be reproduced or transmitted in any form or by any means, electronic or mechanical, including photocopying, recording or by any information storage and retrieval system, without prior written permission from the author, except in the case of brief quotations embodied in critical reviews and certain other noncommercial uses permitted by copyright law.

First Edition March 2017

ISBN-13: 978-0692859490
ISBN-10: 0692859497

Disclaimer: This book is not intended as a substitute for the medical advice of physicians. The reader should regularly consult a physician in matters relating to his/her health and particularly with respect to any symptoms that may require diagnosis or medical attention. Before beginning any new diet or exercise program it is recommended that you seek medical advice from your personal physician. If you have any medical conditions, check with your doctor before performing any kind of detox. Hot baths are not recommended for people with high blood pressure.

Spiritual Beliefs: There are a myriad of cultures and spiritual orientations that use different words to express an understanding of the miracle of consciousness or existence. In this book, this understanding is expressed with different words and phrases such as, "Source", "Divine" or "Spirit". I encourage you to use the terminology that suits your beliefs best.

DEDICATION

This book is dedicated to anyone wants to live more, love deeper and be happier. Cheers to you!

CONTENTS

Acknowledgments	i
Introduction	1
How to Use this Book	2
Week One	4
Week Two	45
Week Three	64
Week Four	88
Week Five	106
Week Six	121
Week Seven	141
Week Eight	157

ACKNOWLEDGMENTS

Thank you to the following individuals for their support:

Lisa Nicole
Rachel Eva
Liz Dawn
Integrative Wellness Academy
Mishka Productions

& The Love of my Life, William

INTRODUCTION

Welcome to Release Density & Shift Your Life: The Companion Workbook! I initially created the Release Density & Shift Your Life online coaching program after friends and family were constantly asking me about a recent and unplanned weight loss. I was always a curvy girl, at times my weight fluctuations bordering on obese, but this time I hadn't really started dieting or exercising more than I had previously had. I was starting to pay attention to what I was putting into my body (food, drink and thought) and what I was holding in my body and not releasing from it (physically and energetically). For the first time in my life, stubborn belly fat start to shift that had never budged even after years of dieting, exercising and crazy weight loss fads. I knew that the weight was slipping off because I had started to listen to my body, to what my soul knew that it needed. I was also doing the emotional work that I had avoided for a long time – the stuff that no one wants to go back and deal with, the thoughts, feelings and emotions that were shoved in the recesses of my mind, filed away until such a time I was able to process and handle them properly, and with the respect they deserved. By identifying and removing all the things in my life that were no longer serving my highest and best good, I was able to release myself from what was holding me back from creating the life of my dreams.

When I first started to create the Release Density & Shift Your Life program, I thought that it was supposed to be for weight loss, but as time went on and the group progressed further and further into the material, I started to realize that it wasn't about weight loss – it was about finding purpose, truth and happiness. What I wanted to do was show others all of the tools at their disposal for getting in tune with themselves and creating the life they want. This book was created after the rising popularity of my online life coaching program of the same name. In creating a companion book to the online group coaching program, I wanted to allow people to start to Release Density & Shift Their Lives *on their own terms*, not just when I was leading a group. I want people to empower themselves as they learn more about their bodies and the amazing things that they are capable of doing! I am honored to be this journey of health and wellness with you. Thank you and Namaste!

HOW TO USE THIS BOOK

This book serves as the companion workbook to the Release Density & Shift Your Life online program. The book contains all of the written assignments and class notes that are provided during the 8-week program. Each week has a different theme, which will include assignments honoring the subject(s). Each weekly "module" has at least seven activities, presumably so that one can be completed for each day of the week. As I tell all of my clients, you will get out of the program what you choose to put in. If you pick and choose the assignments that seem "easy" to you, or just do one or two per week, you will not get the most out of your experience. If you are in the online group and you do not do the selected assignments for the week, you will not get the most out of your experience. Now I will say, you always get exactly what you need, but this is about pushing yourself out of your comfort zone to get the most from this experience. Your healing and your transformation is 100% within your control. As a life coach, I am here to give you the tools, guidance and support, but you need to make the commitment to yourself to do the work. As in the online group, I strongly recommend having an accountability buddy to check in with and help motivate you along your journey to wellness. If you are the type of person who prefers more structure and accountability, you may consider the Release Density & Shift Your Life program online. Benefits of this group include:

- 8 one-hour live group coaching sessions
- 30 minute personalized guidance session with Arielle Sterling
- Basic DNA reprogramming (I love myself, I forgive myself, I am worthy)
- Membership to a private Facebook group for ongoing daily support
- Special access to member's only page on Arielle Sterling's website
- 25% off any services that Arielle Sterling offers during your 8 week program
- Lifetime access to materials, recorded group coaching videos PLUS any new materials created for the program

Please see my website, www.ariellesterling.com for more information and to check the next group start date!

WEEK ONE
INTRODUCTIONS

I invite you to take this week to reintroduce you to yourself. Your true self. The person that you are underneath the clothes, the makeup, all of the messiness and all of the stress. This week you will be doing a series of self-assessments so that you can gain an awareness of where you are at on a number of different levels: mental, emotional, physical and spiritual.

- Holistic Self Assessment: General (5)
- Holistic Self Assessment: Physical (11)
- Holistic Self Assessment: Emotional (22)
- Holistic Self Assessment: Mental (25)
- Holistic Self Assessment: Spiritual (27)
- Goal Brainstorming (28)
- SMART Goals (30)
- Daily Tracker (31)
- Mind, Body, Spirit Self Care (32)
- Authentic Happiness Inventory (34)

RELEASE DENSITY & SHIFT YOUR LIFE

HOLISTIC SELF ASSESSMENT: General

What are the reasons (problems, challenges, circumstances) that you want to shift?

_____
_____
_____
_____

The problems I need help with are:

_____
_____
_____
_____

On a scale of 1-10 how intensely do you experience this problem (how 'big'/'bad' is it), 10 being the most intense, 1 being the least.

|—————————————————————————|
1   2   3   4   5   6   7   8   9   10

What have you done so far to try to resolve the problem? List any action steps you have taken.

_____
_____
_____
_____

List why or how these problems effect your life (why are they a problem?):

_____
_____
_____
_____

How long has this been a problem or struggle in your life?

_____
_____
_____
_____

When was it not?

_____
_____
_____
_____

What specifically created this problem? What steps led to it?

_____
_____
_____
_____

How do you feel about the problem (what emotions are present)?

_____
_____
_____
_____

Tell about your family and childhood as it relates to the current situation (what is the relationship between your past experiences/people and the current problem):

_____
_____
_____
_____
_____

Is there a purpose or a reason for having this problem?

_____
_____
_____
_____
_____

How will you know when the problem has totally disappeared (what will that look like or feel like)?

_____
_____
_____
_____
_____

How will it feel/look like in your life when the problem is gone?

_____
_____
_____
_____
_____

Are you willing to take the steps necessary in order to release the problem from your life/resolve the problem?

_____

On a scale of 1-10 how committed are you willing to be with your time, energy and resources towards overcoming this problem. 1 being the least committed and 10 being the most.

|—|—|—|—|—|—|—|—|—|—|
1   2   3   4   5   6   7   8   9   10

My biggest goals are:

_____
_____
_____
_____

The areas I struggle most in are:

_____
_____
_____
_____

I spend most of my time on (or doing):

_____
_____
_____
_____

I spend a lot of time on thinking about:

_____
_____
_____
_____

My definition of success is:

_____
_____
_____
_____

My definition of wellness and health is:
_____
_____
_____
_____

What area of your life would you most like to improve (health, relationships, family, finances, career, spirituality or self development?
_____
_____
_____
_____

What areas are your areas of struggle example of main areas: family, relationships, career, finances, health, spirituality, self awareness/self development)?
_____
_____
_____
_____

Do you struggle to find balance between your fitness needs, personal needs, life tasks, social life and work? If yes, when time is tight, which is the first area you cut down on?
_____
_____
_____
_____

What do you find most challenging in life (relationships, work, money, family, etc.)?
_____
_____
_____
_____

What is more challenging for you, balance or discipline?
_____
_____

What areas would you like to see healing/growth in?
_____
_____
_____
_____

What are some of the things that you feel limit you in growth or block you from living to your fullest ability?

_____
_____
_____
_____

What are you most passionate about in life? Do you feel that you are living your purpose?

_____
_____
_____
_____

What would you like to feel or be different, better or more in your life?

_____
_____
_____
_____

What would you like to have, be or do more in your life?

_____
_____
_____
_____

What do you think is the most beautiful or positive thing about the world? The worst?

_____
_____
_____
_____

What are you most grateful for in your life?

_____
_____
_____
_____

When you have had a long day and really need to 'recharge' would you choose to be home and have some alone time or go out and socially interact?

_____
_____
_____
_____

When you experience stress, negative feelings and or emotions what do you typically do to deal with them? Or what do you do to avoid feeling uncomfortable? How do you escape or process them (please list both positive and negative ways you do this)?

RELEASE DENSITY & SHIFT YOUR LIFE

HOLISTIC SELF ASSESSMENT: Physical

Nutrition

Write down your average daily food intake (meals and what they are made up of as well as what time of the day):

_____
_____
_____
_____
_____
_____

What do you think your biggest struggle, challenge, issue or problem is in the area of food/nutrition for you? What do you feel are your biggest challenges with diet and nutrition?

_____
_____
_____
_____

Where (what stores or markets) do you purchase groceries from?

_____
_____
_____

How often do you eat dairy products?

_____
_____

How often do you eat grain & wheat products (bread, rice, pasta, etc.)?

_____
_____

What is your guilty pleasure (food or drink)?

_____
_____
_____

What favorite foods/drinks can you not live without?

_____
_____
_____

What foods do you really like?

_____
_____
_____
_____

What foods do you really dislike or have a negative reaction to?

_____
_____
_____
_____

What is your favorite meal?

_____
_____
_____
_____

When do you crave your favorite things (night time, on weekends, etc.)?

_____
_____
_____
_____

How often do you eat potato chips, corn chips or similar snack foods?

_____
_____
_____
_____

How often, how much and what kind of alcohol do you consume?

_____
_____
_____
_____

How many servings or fruit do you eat every day?

_____
_____
_____
_____

How many servings of vegetables do you eat every day?

_____
_____
_____
_____

What sources and how much protein do you eat every day (fish, chicken, eggs, meat, whey protein powder, etc.)?

_____
_____
_____

How many servings of grains (rice, oatmeal, breads, pasta, etc.) do you eat per day and what kind?

_____
_____
_____

How much water (how many 8 oz. glasses) do you consume per day?

_____
_____
_____

Which describes what your typically eating habit is; stop eating when you feel full, when your plate is empty, go back for a second helping, or forget to eat frequently?

_____
_____
_____

Do you typically eat quickly, normal speed or slowly?

_____
_____

Are you satisfied with your sex life?

_____
_____
_____

How many times per day do you eat?

_____
_____
_____

How many sweets (candy, sugar, deserts) do you eat per day?

How many of your daily meals have condiments or dressings on them?

How often do you eat canned, pre-prepared or frozen foods? What kinds?

How many times per week do you eat out?

How many caffeinated beverages (coffee, tea, soda) do you drink per day and what kind?

Fitness

What do you feel are your biggest challenges with exercise?
_____
_____
_____
_____

How often do you exercise and for how long each session?
_____
_____
_____
_____

How long have you been exercising and are you consistent?
_____
_____
_____
_____

Did you or do you play any sports? Did you play sports in high school or college?
_____
_____
_____
_____

What physical activities do you most enjoy (dancing, biking, hiking, surfing, etc.)?
_____
_____
_____
_____

What hobbies do you enjoy in life or what things do like to do/want to do for fun (can be physical or non physical)?
_____
_____
_____
_____

What do you least enjoy about exercise?

What areas of your body do you feel are your strongest?

What areas of the body do you feel are your weakest?

What areas of the body do you want to see the most change in?

Would you characterize your cardiovascular ability as good, average or poor?

Would you characterize your flexibility as good, average or poor?

Do you start exercise programs and find it is hard to stick to them or to continue them after a period of time?

What is the biggest reason, challenge or goal that brought you to seek out help?

What is your biggest or most important goal to achieve in your fitness?

Personal & Family History

What would you like to be different, better or more in your physical world (health, fitness, nutrition, and/or things you have in your life)?

_____
_____
_____
_____

Please write a brief bullet point medical & personal & family history. Please also include dates next to any illness, injury, major life change or loss. Please make sure to list any medical conditions and medications (include dosage):

_____
_____
_____
_____
_____
_____
_____
_____

What is your genetic as well as cultural background (please list both sides of the family and their approximate year of birth. Example: African American (father), Middle Eastern (mother), culturally raised in middle eastern environment (food, traditions, etc.), grew up in Nebraska).

_____
_____
_____
_____

Please describe your current state of health in your physical body:

_____
_____
_____
_____

Do you smoke cigarettes or use drugs, if so how many/much and how often?

_____
_____
_____
_____

Do you have high blood pressure or high cholesterol?
_____
_____

When did you last have blood work done? Was everything normal?
_____
_____
_____
_____

Date of last physical?
_____

Date of last eye exam?
_____

Date of last dental exam/cleaning?
_____

Do you think that you are over weight? If so, by how much?
_____
_____
_____
_____

History of mental illness or depression (you or your family, including those you live with)?
_____
_____
_____
_____

Any family members with mental illness, depression, heart disease, diabetes, cancer, obesity, eating disorders, other diseases, illnesses or conditions?
_____
_____
_____
_____
_____
_____

Do you take vitamins and/or supplements, if so, what kind and how often?
_____
_____
_____
_____

Are you on any medication (please list dosage & info in detail again here)?

Have you been diagnosed with any illnesses, diseases or disorders?

Have you ever received any advice or warnings regarding physical exercise by a doctor? If so what?

Life Habits

How many days and hours per week do you work?

___

Do you enjoy your job? If yes, what specifically about it do you enjoy. If no, what specifically about it do you find unsatisfying? Do you feel that you are doing what you are called & created you to do aka 'living your dream'?

___

How many hours per night do you sleep?

___

How often do you go on vacation? When was your last vacation, where was it and how long were you there?

___

How much time do you spend out doors? When out doors, what activities (walking the dog, gardening, going to the beach, outdoor cafes, etc.)?

___

HOLISTIC SELF ASSESSMENT: Emotional

What would you like to be different, better or more in your emotional life (feelings, emotions, relationships - with self and others)?

_____
_____
_____
_____

Would you consider your upbringing healthy or dysfunctional? Why?

_____
_____
_____
_____

Who do you spend most of your time with? Is that relationship satisfying?

_____
_____
_____
_____

What is your activity level in your community? Do you have a group of friends you see regularly?

_____
_____
_____
_____

Have you ever experienced physical, emotional, verbal, spiritual or sexual abuse?

_____
_____
_____
_____

What recreational (enjoyable and relaxing) things do you enjoy? How often do you do them?

_____
_____
_____
_____

What do you like about yourself? What don't you like about yourself?

_____
_____
_____
_____

Do you have negative emotions that you still feel now that have to do with things that have happened in the past?

___

Do you have any anger, resentments or un-forgiveness towards any person, place, thing or situation (including God)?

___

How often to you see or speak to friends?

___

Write a brief description of how you have perceived yourself (your mind, body, etc.) for the majority of your life and any recent changes to that?

___

Write a brief description of your relationship to food and exercise (and self care) in the past and present?

___

Write a brief description of your relationship with yourself in the past and present?

___

Write a brief description of your relationship with others (family, friends, lovers/partners) in the past and present?

___

Do you feel very satisfied, moderately satisfied or dissatisfied with your life most of the time?

Are you single or in a relationship? If you are married, how often do you and your spouse go on dates with each other?

Are you happy with your relationship and/or relationship status? Is it fulfilling? What could make it more fulfilling?

When something upsets you, do you tend to get angry, get sad, get frustrated, shut down, cry, ignore it or talk about it?

What have been the most significant losses and major life changes you have experienced?

When you experienced these losses/changes, what coping tools did you use to deal with them; food, TV, sex, drugs, sleep, alcohol, shutting down/avoidance, shopping, anger, reading, and/or others?

Do you feel satisfied with your personal life?

RELEASE DENSITY & SHIFT YOUR LIFE

HOLISTIC SELF ASSESSMENT: Mental

What top 5 things/characteristics do you most value in life (example; integrity, love, success, money, friendship, support, freedom, etc.)? Please list them in order of importance to you (1 being the highest priority and 5 being the lowest).

1.
2.
3.
4.
5.

Are you more of an optimist or pessimist?

_____
_____
_____
_____

What do you think most about often?

_____
_____
_____
_____

Are your thoughts happy, stressful, sad, etc.?

_____
_____
_____
_____

What would you like to be different, better or more in the 'mental' area of your life (thoughts, patterns, habits and self perceptions)?

_____
_____
_____

When you have thoughts about yourself what are they? When you look in the mirror what do you usually think?

_____
_____
_____
_____

How often do you learn new things through reading, researching, taking classes or seminars or having discussions with others?

When you spend time thinking about you and your life, what feeling (either physically or emotionally) do you feel afterwards (example: anxious, stressed, happy, positive, hopeful, empowered, helpless, out of control, sick to stomach, headache, exhaustion, overwhelmed, neutral - no different)?

HOLISTIC SELF ASSESSMENT: Spiritual

What are your spiritual beliefs?
_____
_____
_____
_____

Do you have any negative association to any spiritual or religious experiences in the past?
_____
_____
_____
_____

How do you choose to practice your beliefs?
_____
_____
_____
_____

How often do you pray?
_____
_____
_____
_____

How often do you meditate?
_____
_____
_____
_____

How do you think your spiritual life could be strengthened?
_____
_____
_____
_____

What would you like to be different, better or more in your spiritual life?
_____
_____
_____
_____

GOAL BRAINSTORMING

What would your perfect life look like to you? Feel like? Taste like? Sound like? Who is with you?
_____
_____
_____
_____
_____
_____

What have you always wanted to be, do, or have, but you've never started?
_____
_____
_____
_____
_____
_____

Who or what do you wish you had more time for in your life?
_____
_____
_____
_____
_____
_____

What does it mean to be happy? How important is it for you to be happy?
_____
_____
_____
_____
_____
_____

What brings you joy and happiness?
_____
_____
_____
_____
_____
_____

What makes you feel good? What activities do you regularly practice that bring you happiness, energy, and contentment?

_____
_____
_____
_____
_____
_____

What areas of your life don't feel right? What activities make you feel bad—for example, angry, irritated, bored, frustrated or anxious?

_____
_____
_____
_____
_____
_____

In what areas of your life do you find progress, learning, challenge, improvement, and increased mastery?

_____
_____
_____
_____
_____
_____

What would your life look like if everything were working? Be creative!

_____
_____
_____
_____
_____
_____

SMART GOALS

Are you setting yourself up for success? Start by determining what makes a SMART goal...

S   Specific
- How specific is your goal?
- Is your goal significant?
- Is your goal a stretch for you?

M   Measurable
- Is your goal measurable?
- Is your goal meaningful?
- Is your goal motivational?

A   Attainable
- Is your goal attainable?
- It your goal achievable?
- Is your goal action-oriented?

R   Realistic
- Is your goal realistic?
- Is your goal rewarding?
- Is your goal results-oriented?

T   Timed
- Is your goal traceable?
- Is your goal timed?
- Is your goal tangible?

Now, what are you setting out to accomplish?

S	Specific	
M	Measurable	
A	Attainable	
R	Realistic	
T	Timed	

DAILY TRACKER

Use this daily tracker to keep tabs on how you are doing each day progressing through your goals. Download more copies of this worksheet from my website here: http://bit.ly/rddailytracker. Use coupon code "RDSYL" to print out unlimited copies so that you can use this tracker daily.

MIND, BODY, SPIRIT SELF CARE

Use the Mind, Body, Spirit Self Care ideas in conjunction with your Daily Tracker under the "Honor Thyself" section. Pick one mind, one body, and one spirit activity each day to nourish your whole self. Feel free to add your own ideas to the list!

Mind	- Watch a TED Talk - Read a book for personal pleasure - Journal mindfully for at least 10 minutes - Read an inspiring article (NOT NEWS) - Do a puzzle (crossword, Sudoku, etc.) - Practice playing a musical instrument - Research or learn something new (Coursera, Khan Academy, etc.) - DO something new - GO somewhere new - Brainstorm ideas / Goal planning - Read, watch TV or speak in your non-native language - Mindful coloring - Turn off electronics for at least ONE hour (cell, TV, radio, etc.) - De-clutter for 10 minutes - Do something you've been putting off - Plan ahead for tomorrow - clothes, accessories & food - Compliment yourself - Unplug at least ONE hour before bedtime - _____ - _____ - _____ - _____ - _____
Body	- 15 minute workout (breaking a sweat) - Take a brisk walk or jog - Drink a full glass of water upon waking - Drink hot lemon water before eating breakfast - Drink 1-2 Tbsp. Apple Cider Vinegar with at least 8 oz. water before meal - Power Up Smoothie - 7 Minute New York Times Workout - Morning Stretching - Yoga - At least one serving fruit AND veggies with breakfast - Dance for 10 minutes to your favorite music - Eat a mindful meal - Give yourself a foot or hand massage - Apply a face masque - Apply a hair masque

	- Cook a healthy meal - Take a shower - Take a detox bath - Self-Reiki - Balance chakras - Use essential oils - Play cell phone game designed to get you moving (Zombie Run, Pokémon Go, etc.) - Go Geocaching - Garden outside - _____ - _____ - _____ - _____ - _____
Spirit	- Set daily intentions - Meditate - Practice mindfulness - Do a random act of kindness (for a spouse, co-worker, stranger, etc.) - Write a poem - Reach out to someone who has been on your mind - Write a letter - Play with an animal - Express gratitude - Sit outside and commune with nature - Sit with crystals and feel their energy - Watch your favorite movie (YES, AGAIN!) - Turn on your favorite song/album and SING at the top of your lungs - Light a candle - Create a vision board - Laugh! Turn on your favorite show or comedian! - Pull oracle/tarot cards - Jump on your bed - Make a pillow fort - Go to a Farmers Market - _____ - _____ - _____ - _____ - _____

AUTHENTIC HAPPINESS INVENTORY

It's a good idea to complete various kinds of self assessments in order to see where you are at, and then in time, to see the progress you have made. Happiness is one of the things that we desire most, yet often do so little to achieve. Let's see where you are at with your own happiness.

- Please visit the University of Pennsylvania's Authentic Happiness website at:
  https://www.authentichappiness.sas.upenn.edu
  (You will need to create a log in)
- Under "Questionnaires" you will find the "Authentic Happiness Inventory"
- Please take this survey and answer the following questions

Are you surprised by your score?

_____
_____
_____
_____

Do you feel that you answered the questions authentically or based on your current mood?

_____
_____
_____
_____

How happy are you compared to others in your profession? Your area?

_____
_____
_____
_____

How did this inventory change your thinking about happiness?

_____
_____
_____
_____

Any other reflections?

_____
_____
_____
_____

RELEASE DENSITY & SHIFT YOUR LIFE

WEEK OF:

MY GOAL THIS WEEK IS:

I WILL ACCOMPLISH MY GOAL THIS WEEK BY TAKING THESE ACTIONS:
01.
02.
03.

HABIT	S	M	T	W	T	F	S
8+ GLASSES H2O							
5+ SERVINGS FRUIT & VEGGIES							
LEAN PROTEIN ONLY							
HOMEMADE FOOD ONLY							
NATURAL SUGARS ONLY							
ALCOHOL FREE							
SWEATY MOVEMENT							
MIND							
BODY							
SPIRIT							

Release Density & Shift Your Life!

WEEK TWO
WHAT IS NO LONGER SERVING YOU?

Last week's assignments were pure introspection., taking a deep dive into every aspect of your self: mental, emotional, physical and spiritual. I wanted you to be able to see where you are objectively and without the emotion that we as humans so often find ourselves trapped in. Now that you have an idea of where you are presently, you can take some steps to assess what is in your life that is no longer serving your highest and best potential at this time. This week's tasks will bring you a deeper sense of awareness and comprehension of the choices and the power that you have in your own life.

This excerpt from my first book *Shift Happens!: 21 Days to Better Energy Through the Chakras* discusses the connection between the physical and energetic bodies.

> "Chakras act as a part of the subtle energy (non-physical) body and serve as the connection portals from the energy body to specific spots on physical body. Think of a chakra like a faucet, if the chakra is obstructed, it can impede the flow of energy causing blockages and lead to decreased or even no chakra function at all. Pain, discomfort and dis-ease in the physical body are often found where energy is blocked or stagnant in the energetic body. Allowing life force energy to properly flow throughout and around our bodies is what keeps us alive and healthy."

Understanding this is important when taking about the idea of density. When there is dense energy surrounding you, you will often feel tired, sluggish, emotionally drained, unhappy, uneasy, etc. Anything that does not feel good or natural to you is likely dense energy. If there is something (or someone) that is not in alignment with you and your energy, it will feel dense and uncomfortable. That may manifest as feelings of awkwardness, pressure or tightness in your chest, or anxiety. Dense energy can cloud our thoughts, feelings, and emotions as well as cause pain in the body and if left untreated, can remain stagnant where it can manifest into long-term health risks and disease.

This week's combination of readings, assignments and self reflection, will help you to figure out what is no longer serving you. In order to move the energy and release it from your body, here are some methods that may work for you:

- Breathing – Inhalation and exhalation with intention can be one of the best tools to isolate and move energy through the physical and emotional bodies.
- Burning – This technique uses fire to physically transform paper transmuting any energy stored on the paper. When burning, please make sure you are doing this in a safe location (outside, not near any flammable objects, etc.)
- Burping – This is a natural bodily reaction when gas is created in your stomach and/or intestines when your body breaks down food into energy.
- Coughing – A common reflexive action that usually takes place involuntarily to remove any foreign irritants from the system.
- Crying – The shedding of tears reduces stress by releasing a build up hormones.
- Defecating – The physical removal of excrement from the body. The body naturally removes what it cannot process.
- Exercising – This is an intentional release of energy from the body. Different exercises have varied affects on the amount and type of energy moved and released from the body.
- Laughing – One of the best natural medicines, this spontaneous activity can help change your mood immediately.
- Menstruating – This is a woman's body natural way of cleansing and removing tissue from the body.
- Orgasm – This is one of the most fun ways to move energy (but please of course do this in a safe manner that does not harm you in any way)
- Passing Gas – A natural bodily function that occurs when your body creates flatulence while processing food from your stomach and/or intestines.
- Perspiring – Sweating helps to physically remove toxins from your body. This can be done in a manner of ways including exercise, sauna, steam room, detox baths, etc.
- Screaming – This is a raw release of energy and emotions allowing the truth to be heard
- Sneezing – This is a sudden and involuntary release from the nasal passages to clear out an irritation in the nostrils
- Talking – This is an underrated source of release., whether planned or spontaneous, talking can

help move through problems and help with comprehension and understanding.
- Throwing Up – Though this is not the ideal way of moving energy, it is a natural reaction to being stressed out.
- Urinating – This is the bodies natural way of flushing liquid out of the system that it no longer has a use for.
- Writing – This is a fantastic way of removing things from your head that you are ruminating upon.

Before you begin your assignments for the this week, there are some things I want you to start considering for yourself in regards to what is no longer serving you:
- Work – Does your paycheck/benefits outweigh the negatives? Does your job nourish your soul?
- Relationships (Friendship, Romantic or Familial) – Is this a mutually beneficial relationship or is it one-sided?
- Habits – Why are you doing what you're doing? Are you doing something because "that's the way its always been"?
- Situations – What do you get in return? Is there an equal exchange of energy?

If your reactions to the questions above weren't what you had hoped for, don't let your reactions to those questions discourage you. Please consider the follow thoughts:
- You have to put yourself first. You cannot pour from an empty cup.
- Everything happens for a reason. Don't judge yourself for where you're at. You don't know what you don't know. You were supposed to be in that space to learn a lesson or gain something. Now that you are gaining awareness to the situation, it is your choice on how you'd like to move forward (or conversely, not).
- Once you have the awareness to the situation, you can start to pull your energy back to begin recalibration. Trust that the Universe has your back and that everything works out exactly as it should and in the time that it should.

Does any of this leave you in a space of feeling guilty? Enabling others physically, emotionally, energetically or financially stops them from achieving their full potential. We cannot assume that we know what is best for another person, even those that are closest to us, including spouses, children, siblings even parents. Everyone has a unique path that is theirs to walk in this lifetime. For us to think we know what is best for someone else is just conceited, no matter what our connection is to them. If we do not want other people to infringe on our path, we must also extend the same grace and patience to others.

What is it that you are taking on from others around you?
- Physically – Do you find that you get sympathy headaches or nausea when someone else around you feels those things? Are you doing things for someone that is not your responsibility?
- Emotionally – Do you take on other people's emotions? Are you stressed out after talking to someone who is stressed? Angry after talking to someone who is angry?
- Financially – Are you paying for things that are not your responsibility?

What is within the realm of your control?
- Your beliefs
- Your attitude
- Your choices
- Your thoughts
- Your responses
- Your perspective
- How honest you are
- Who your friends are
- What books you read
- How often you exercise
- The type of food you eat
- How many risks you take
- How you interpret situations
- How kind you are to others
- How kind you are to yourself
- How often you say "I Love You"
- How often you say "Thank You"
- How you express your feelings
- Whether or not you ask for help
- How often you practice gratitude

- How many times you smile today
- The amount of effort you put forth
- How you spend/invest your money
- How much time you spend worrying
- How often you think about your past
- Whether or not you judge other people (or yourself)
- Whether or not you try again after a setback
- How much you appreciate the things you have

There are a few more things to consider in the grander scheme how you're letting the world affect you:
- Sports – How wrapped up do you get emotionally with your favorite sports team? Does it stress you out when they play poorly? Do you become physically ill or angry when they lose a game? This is a common obsession that we as a society have created, an intense emotional connection that often takes over rational thought. Major league sports are something that the general population has zero control over, yet people gamble money on, become highly emotional over and even create preconceived notions about other team's fans based on their choice of team.
- Social Media - These feeds are crafted to portray picture perfect snapshots of how people would like their lives to be perceived by others who have access to view their profiles. Social media often does not show the messy, frustrating, daily struggles that everyone experiences, just the unflawed photos and random check-ins flaunting their trips and voyages. Don't let yourself get trapped in the cycle of comparing yourself to others.
- Other People – How are you letting other people affect you? Do you take what other people say to heart? Are you bothered by other people's actions and/or reactions? To paraphrase one of my teachers "other people's opinions of me are none of my business".

ASSIGNMENTS:
- Shift List (51)
- Digital Detox (52)
- What is no longer serving you? (53)
- Sacred Spaces (54)
- Closet Clearing (55)

- Bathroom Sweep (56)
- What are you carrying with you? (57)

SHIFT LIST

Instructions: There are things that you don't like that you do or that you complain about to your partner or friends. List 10 things that you don't want so we can get clear on where your energy is. Now, you are going to shift each statement into a positive statement that reflects what you do want.

EX: I don't want to be judged. SHIFT TO: Other people's opinions of me are not my concern.

1.
Shift to:

2.
Shift to:

3.
Shift to:

4.
Shift to:

5.
Shift to:

6.
Shift to:

7.
Shift to:

8.
Shift to:

9.
Shift to:

10.
Shift to:

DIGITAL DETOX

Instructions: There is so much heaviness, density and frustration lodged in social media. For this assignment, I ask that you go through any social media profiles of yours (Facebook, Twitter, Instagram, etc.) and complete the following tasks:

- Unfollow - Unfollow pages or anyone on social media who you do not align with or does not bring you joy from what they post. A person won't know that you don't see their posts, but you will still remain "friends". I believe that it is an important part of controlling what information is coming into you without your consent, which can almost feel like an assault on the system.

- Unfriend - Completely unfriend someone instead of just unfollowing them if they leave rude or obnoxious comments on your posts. Also, unfriend anyone that you "hate follow" or follow to "keep tabs on them". Keep people on your friends list who you genuinely care about and choose to have in your life and digital space.

- Delete Contacts - Go through your cell phone and email contacts and delete old contact information that you no longer use. You'll be surprised at how much lighter energetically your phone will feel afterwards!

- Remove Old Stuff - Clear up digital AND energetic space by removing old apps from your digital devices that you no longer use. Go through your computer and delete old files, projects and programs.

- Take Some Time Off - There is nothing wrong with detaching yourself from your digital devices, enjoying your surroundings and becoming present with yourself! Start by setting a timer on your phone for at least 15 minutes and challenge yourself to not look at your device during that time.

- It's Okay to Say "No" - Do not feel obligated to accept every friend or follow request on your social media accounts. Be conscientious of whose energy you choose to allow to infiltrate your social media.

What changes did you notice?

_____

_____

Any resistance to removing people?

_____

_____

WHAT IS NO LONGER SERVING YOU?

Instructions: Often times we do things that do not serve our highest and best good, purely out of a sense of obligation to others. The only obligation that we truly hold is to ourselves. After all, we cannot help others if we are not taking care of ourselves first. Think about 10 things that you do that are no longer serving you and list them below.

1. _____

2. _____

3. _____

4. _____

5. _____

6. _____

7. _____

8. _____

9. _____

10. _____

Are you ready to start honoring yourself? Take a deep breath in and exhale, letting go of anything that no longer serves you. Often times awareness is enough to change the energy of the situation and allow you to move forward into healing. Copy this list onto a clean sheet of paper and burn it SAFELY to release what is no longer serving you.

SACRED SPACES

Instructions: Take a look at the spaces that you spend the most time in: kitchen, office, bedroom? How do they feel to you? Are they cluttered? Do they honor your personality? Take at least 10 minutes today to de-clutter each space that you spend considerable time in. Try and create "Sacred Spaces" around your home or office that promote your health and happiness. An example of this may be a small collection of crystals, a salt lamp, a plant or succulent, or trinkets that make you happy.

How did this task feel?

_____
_____
_____
_____
_____
_____
_____

Was it easy or hard to do? Why or why not?

_____
_____
_____
_____
_____
_____
_____

What changes did you notice in your space?

_____
_____
_____
_____
_____
_____
_____

CLOSET CLEARING

Instructions: When is the last time you went through your closet and actually took a look at what you have in there? Are there items Are you holding onto a range of sizes wide enough to fill a whole store? Get rid of them! They are cluttering your energetic space! Your task today is to spend at least 5 minutes going through your:

- Clothes
- Sweaters
- Shoes
- Purses/accessories

Remove the items that you don't like, that are old and tattered, that are out of style, do not fit properly or are just ugly (we've all bought something and had near immediate buyers remorse, right?)

Throw them out if the quality has been compromised, but if they are still in relatively good condition you have a number of options of disposal:

- Consignment shop
- Donation (Goodwill, homeless shelter, women's shelter, etc.)
- Clothing swap party with friends and family (donate what is left afterwards)

If it doesn't seem like a lot, that's okay, don't hold yourself in a space of judgment. Start to ask yourself what you really use and why you are holding onto things if you are not using them. Is there a void that you are trying to fill with material goods? A good way to see what you actually use from your closet is to turn your hangers so that they are all facing one direction. When you use a garment of clothing, turn the hanger the other direction. After a month, two months or even three months, take a look and see what hasn't moved in your closet. This will give you a more realistic idea of what you are using and not using and give you stronger reason to consider removing the item.

BATHROOM SWEEP

Instructions: Similar to the other assignments this week, I challenge you to take a look at your bathroom and go through your personal care products and identify what you have on hand and what you are using that is helpful and remove the rest. Please take at least 10 minutes today and go through any old or expired products that are discolored or smell spoiled, or that you no longer like or are using. Be sure to check all of these:

- Toiletries (toothpaste, deodorant, etc.)
- Self care products (lotion, shaving cream, etc.)
- Makeup / cosmetics (including nail polishes)
- Hair products (shampoo, conditioner, hair spray, etc.)
- Perfumes
- Sample sizes / hotel samples
- Medicine cabinets
- Bathroom drawers

What patterns did you notice?

_____
_____
_____
_____
_____

What, if any, resistance showed up during this activity?

_____
_____
_____
_____
_____

WHAT ARE YOU CARRYING WITH YOU?

Instructions: So many of us carry the same items with us day after day without conscientiously considering the energy of what we are carrying. Women often carry purses overstuffed with pens, receipts, change, and random miscellanea. Men often carry wallets that can grow to over an inch in width stuffed with items that are not always vital to be carried around. Students and commuters often carry backpacks that collect generous amounts of items due to their size. People drive around in cars littered with trash, dirty clothes and papers, so today I want you to ask yourself what are you carrying with you? Take at least 10 minutes for this task and go through any (or all) of these spaces, purging of what is no longer useful to you:

- Wallet
- Purse
- Briefcase
- Backpack
- Diaper bag
- Car – Visible interior
    - Center console
    - Glove compartment
    - Trunk

What was this task like for you?

_____
_____
_____
_____
_____

What did you notice? Any patterns?

_____
_____
_____
_____
_____

WEEK OF:

MY GOAL THIS WEEK IS:

I WILL ACCOMPLISH MY GOAL THIS WEEK BY TAKING THESE ACTIONS:
01.

02.

03.

HABIT	S	M	T	W	T	F	S
8+ GLASSES H20							
5+ SERVINGS FRUIT & VEGGIES							
LEAN PROTEIN ONLY							
HOMEMADE FOOD ONLY							
NATURAL SUGARS ONLY							
ALCOHOL FREE							
SWEATY MOVEMENT							
MIND							
BODY							
SPIRIT							

Release Density & Shift Your Life!

WEEK THREE
BODY + NATURE

We are only given one body in this lifetime, so learning to work with it instead of against it is paramount. Once we begin to honor our own uniqueness, we can stop fighting ourselves and figure out what we really need, not only to survive, but to thrive! As Socrates said, "to know thyself is the beginning of wisdom" and that is what this week is about! You are the only one who knows what is best for your body. It will tell you if it does not like what is happening to it! If you consume something (food, drink, medicine, etc.) and you feel:

- tired
- bloated
- itchy (including rashes)
- aches or pain
- cramps
- diarrhea or constipation

then your body is trying to tell you something! The body is intelligent enough to know what is good for it and what isn't! Are you listening to it?

Let's talk about your relationship with food. How do you view food? Are you eating to nourish body? Or are you eating what ever is quick, easy and convenient? Ask yourself about the way you view sustenance and nutrition:

- What time of day do you eat? – Are you eating at the same time each day, consuming breakfast, lunch and dinner similar to a typical American diet? Or are you listening to body's own needs, eating as your body signals that it is hungry?
- What is fueling you? – Are you eating processed and diet foods trying to "eat healthy"? Or are you eating organic, non-GMO fresh food that has not been changed from it's original form? Are you refueling your body with pure, unadulterated water? Or are you drinking chemical-laden
- How did your ancestors eat? – The human body was not created to process chemicals, non-natural

ingredients and most items that have been created or altered by humans! Think about the way cultures have eaten for hundreds of thousands of years when looking for inspiration. Diet shakes, low-fat items and sugar-free options are all examples of created constructs that pretend to be healthy.

The process of digestion is one of the highest usages of energy in the body, which is why you feel tired after a large or heavy meal; this is the body is actually struggling to process what has been put into it, so it shuts down other non-vital functions in order to digest properly. What we put into our bodies is what we get out. If you are eating food that your body is struggling to process, it will hinder the body's natural ability to heal itself. By eating food that is organic and non-GMO, your body isn't fighting through chemicals and toxins to process the nourishment it needs to gain and doesn't hinder the body's ability to complete routine tasks. Do your best to purchase organic ingredients as they are available and as you can afford them! I would say that this is an area to really consider being proactive with (buying organic foods) versus dealing with future consequences (medical costs). If you can't purchase 100% organic or if it is not available, focus on making sure that you purchase foods that have a soft, permeable skin organically (ex: apples) instead a hard skin (ex: orange). If the skin is to be removed and not consumed, chemicals aren't absorbed (as much) into the flesh of the food that you will eat. Here are some of the most important items to find organic:

- apples
- bell peppers
- blueberries
- celery
- chocolate
- coffee
- collard greens
- cucumbers
- fatty meats
- grapes
- kale
- lettuce
- milk
- nectarines
- peaches

- potato (sweet potato, yam, etc.)
- spinach
- strawberries
- tomatoes
- wine
- zucchini

Before I consume anything, I try and ask myself, "How is this nourishing to my body?" This is a way for me to check into why I am eating what I am eating, and if I am just eating out of boredom or frustration. And there are still times that I continue on with what I am doing even though I logically know it isn't good for me, but at least I'm thinking about it, and not mindlessly acting.

Did you know that your skin is the largest organ in the human body? Think about what you do to that beautiful skin of yours! Maybe you shave it, exfoliate it, slather lotion on it, spray it, soak it, wrap it, but are you considering what chemicals are you allowing to be absorbed through your skin via:

- soap
- lotion
- makeup
- sunscreen
- deodorant

The same concepts of natural, organic, non-GMO ingredients should carry over into your beauty and skin care products and regimen.

ASSIGNMENTS:

- Read "Food" excerpt from *Shift Happens! 21 Days to Better Energy Through the Chakras* (68)
- Read "Water & Hydration" excerpt from *Shift Happens! 21 Days to Better Energy Through the Chakras* (71)
- Read "Exercise" excerpt from *Shift Happens! 21 Days to Better Energy Through the Chakras* (72)
- Body Letter 1 (73)
- Allergy Test (74)
- Mindful Meal (81)
- Watch a Documentary (82)

"FOOD" FROM *SHIFT HAPPENS! 21 DAYS TO BETTER ENERGY THROUGH THE CHAKRAS*

Food is one of the most important aspects of maintaining your personal energy. The old adage of "you are what you eat" is entirely accurate once you come to the understanding that everything is indeed energy. We eat to nourish our bodies, to provide the proper nutrition so that our bodies can continue producing miracles. One of the best things that you can do for yourself is to fuel your body properly, honoring your body as a sacred vessel by choosing healthy, fresh, and natural options.

It took me a long time to come to this understanding and heal my relationship with food. I was raised in an environment where my food intake was restricted. I was told what to eat, when to eat and how to eat it. I didn't put my own food on my plate or make decisions about what I chose to consume. As a result of this, when I went out, I would binge eat, which eventually led to purging. Once I started looking at the emotional aspect of my relationship with food, I was able to release the old beliefs that I was carrying inside me that connected food with guilt, shame and self-loathing. I was able to make the connection that the energy with which we consume the food has everything to do with how our body receives the nutrition of the food. I now understand that food is to be treated as fuel for the body, so that it can achieve its full potential. Food is not a reward or treat, but the vehicle which provides the body sustenance. Recently I have seen an image circulating on social media that perfectly summed up this idea stating, "Stop rewarding yourself with food. You are not a dog."

Cooking beautiful, healthy food has since become one of my passions. I love to challenge myself and see how many nutrient-rich items I can fit into one dish while maintaining a high caliber of execution. I try to buy whole, fresh foods (organic if possible and reasonable!) versus packaged and prepared. I do this for a number of reasons – the first being that I have had food allergies since childhood, so I have had to be consciousness of the ingredients in the food I consume. The second reason is that I like to control the flavor and the spice in my food. Not that I am picky, but there are certain things that I cannot stand in my food (I'm talking to you, cilantro, cumin and coriander). By preparing the majority of my own food, I can maintain that level of quality control that I desire. I also tend to find prepared food too salty for my tastes. Growing up, there was a point in time that I was taking Lithium pills in combination with other treatments for depression. Since taking the Lithium (which is a salt compound), I find my tastes being very sensitive to salt and sodium in food.

Cooking is all about creativity and adaptability. My cooking is entirely guided by intuition; I only use recipes when baking. I don't measure out amounts of ingredients or spices. I have been known to have full conversations with my Spirit guides while cooking, asking for advice on unknown food adventures. I am told that its quite entertaining to watch me cook, bake or fumble with my varied collection of kitchen appliances and utensils. I use what I have, what is readily available and what I am guided to include in a dish. I've made some interesting (and delicious!) food swaps for typical ingredients instead of purchasing a special ingredient. I typically cook a bunch of grains and veggies at once so that I have base ingredients to build from during the week. This way I don't have to work so hard when I am really hungry. I have found that when I don't have options available to throw something together quickly, that is when I turn to food that my stomach quickly regrets. Sometimes a snack for me is as simple as fresh mozzarella cheese with whatever roasted veggies I have in the fridge with a drizzle of balsamic reduction or just a handful of pretzels and dried cranberries. Even when I have food around that I don't love (who decides what flavors go in the 3-pack of yogurt anyways?), I find adding spices and extra love is a fast way to make your food palatable.

I should also mention that I am proponent of eating whatever you want, at the meal that you want. Now I am not saying to go ballistic and eat everything in your line of sight. What I mean is that you shouldn't categorize food only to be eaten at a specific time. If you wake up craving steak, have a steak for breakfast. Listen to your body and what it is telling you that it wants, when it wants. This is not license to go crazy and binge eat whatever you want; what I am asking you to do is check in with what your body wants before you make food choices, not your logical mind. Your body will tell you what it wants if you take the time to listen and honor it. There is no hard and fast rule that says you can only eat cereal between the hours of 5 and 9 am, so there should be nothing stopping you from eating the meal you want, when you want it. And let's be real, if your body does not appreciate what you've eaten it'll tell you!

When making changes in your diet, it is crucial to listen to your body and give it the proper support that it needs, in order to make the shifts that you are asking it to make. I have found out the hard way that for my body, gluten does not work. I had been tested many times for wheat allergies and various related conditions, but there was never any medical confirmation that told me to avoid gluten. Begrudgingly, one day, I listened to a dear friend when she recommended that I try to avoid gluten to see if it helped my stomach ailments. People kept telling me that I should try and eliminate it from my diet, but I was stubborn since I had previously tried to eliminate it for maybe a week at a time with no results. I had never actually stuck with anything long-term, but I was ready to try anything that would help me end my constant pain. Honestly, I didn't notice too much change at first, until I was about two weeks into my gluten-free adventure. I had lunch plans with a girlfriend from college, at one of our favorite hometown restaurants where I would normally go straight for a sandwich. One that would clearly be packed with delicious, delicious gluten. I had asked my guides for a sign that would indicate if I was supposed to indulge in what I wanted, or stick with my new dietary changes. That morning when I got out of the shower, I looked down at my arms and noticed that I was able to see the bones in my hands and the veins in my arms. I know this sounds trivial, but when your body is so consistently inflamed that these features are indistinguishable, it is quite noticeable when they do reappear. Of course, after seeing that I couldn't bring myself to eat a sandwich that day and I was *that person* who ordered a salad in a sandwich joint. Now when I do consume food with gluten, my body reacts almost instantaneously with a headache and upset stomach not far behind.

You may have noticed that there are a number of foods that work in tandem with the root chakra, but the amount of foods that work to balance the chakra decreases as you work your way up to the crown chakra. Building from a strong root, eating a full rainbow of colors will not only help to keep your chakra aligned, it will help you to maintain a healthy lifestyle. Each shade of the rainbow provides benefits of different vibrations, along with the full spectrum of vitamins and minerals that the body needs. The internet is a wonderful source of help when it comes to cooking and meal planning. I have found great success skimming websites like Pinterest for inspiration when I have unfamiliar ingredients. Over the few pages, I will share the foods that work in tandem with each chakra, along some of my favorite breakfasts, lunches, dinners and snack options and ideas that correlate to each. These are all food choices that I would make when I need an extra boost. You will find some space in each section to make note of your favorite foods too! I will be featuring some of the meal idea recipes on my website: www.ariellesterling.com .

"WATER & HYDRATION" FROM *SHIFT HAPPENS! 21 DAYS TO BETTER ENERGY THROUGH THE CHAKRAS*

The human body is composed of at least 50% liquid water at any given time. Every individual is unique, with each bodies composition containing at times up to 75% water (babies and children), decreasing over time as the body transforms. Aside from water being nearly 20% of the blood's plasma, it has a number of vital responsibilities in the body. It is the primary building block of the body's cells (37.2 trillion of them in case you were wondering—I was). Lubricating the joints, water in the body acts as a shock absorber to your organs, in addition to insulating key organs such as the brain and spinal cord. There are many other compounds in the body that utilize water as a component, so there is often debate over how much water the body actually contains. Given this understanding of merely a few of the functions water has in your body, it is much easier to understand why it is so important to consume plenty of water and stay properly hydrated.

The body recognizes thirst after an individual has already lost about 2-3% of their hydration, however mental performance and physical coordination become impaired after a 1% hydration loss. If you are only drinking when you are thirsty, your body is already dehydrated. A lot of people that they don't drink water because they don't like the taste. I grew up in the Chicago area and there is nothing better than the taste of Lake Michigan tap water, but now living in here in Arizona, we don't drink the tap water, so I can appreciate when people say that water has a taste. Nonetheless, it is still important to hydrate properly. I prefer to drink water based drinks such as tea or lemonade versus anything artificially processed like soda, energy or sports drinks. I don't like the idea of added chemicals or dyes being added to anything I consume, so I do my best to stay away from those things.

A great way to add an extra punch of flavor to your water to help encourage regular consumption is to add fresh fruit, herbs or spices. I like constant variety so I tend to use a water bottle with a built in strainer, but feel free to brew a larger batch. This way it is ready for you to drink, and not just when you are thirsty! There is an endless amount of flavor combinations that can be made! Make sure to start with the best ingredients possible to achieve the best outcome: filtered water, the freshest fruit available, fresh herbs and whole spices are preferred. The more ingredients you use and the longer you let your water brew, the more flavorful your water will become. If you're easing into this idea a good place to start is with a neutral and comfortable flavor such as lemon or cucumber. By just letting a slice infuse into a glass of water, you are enjoying the subtle benefits of this chakra energy boost. I have also heard of people adding essential oils to their water, which I think is quite an interesting idea. The only thing I would say is to make sure that you are well versed, making sure that your oil is food grade and meant for human consumption.

"EXERCISE" FROM *SHIFT HAPPENS! 21 DAYS TO BETTER ENERGY THROUGH THE CHAKRAS*

Exercise was my biggest foe, my arch nemesis. When something like exercise and fitness is forced upon you, there can be a certain level of distain that clouds any benefits that you may be receiving from it. Every time I exercised I would be full of anger and resentment, which created layers of anger and resentment trapped in my body. Just like anything else, the energy in which we perform an action is the energy you receive in return, not necessarily the actual prescribed benefits. It took years for me to make this connection, and come to the understanding that exercise had nothing to do with losing weight, as many of us have been brought up to believe. Let me repeat that, exercise has nothing to do with losing weight.

Once I had shifted my perspective on exercise, I came to the understanding that exercise was intended to move energy throughout the body. The excess weight that had been hanging around my middle started to fall off once I made this connection and starting doing the emotional work, not just focusing on the diet and exercise aspects of being healthy. I am not the kind of person who enjoys the gym experience like some people do. Staring at myself in a mirror while I work up a sweat, is not my idea of a fun time, so I tend to gravitate towards outdoor activities. I typically don't exercise with other people, but meeting up with friends to go hiking or walk around a street fair or farmers market never feels forced. The most important thing about exercise is that you find something that you enjoy doing and just do it!

The universe provides us opportunities to do what our bodies need as long as we pay attention to the signs. For example, there are days when I'll ask for exercise to be built into my day and then, mysteriously, there aren't any parking spaces and I'm taking a nice scenic walk. Or those times when we don't want to do squats, but end up having to pull weeds instead, those situations are more than just coincidence. Don't discount those little synchronicities and the universe chiming in as to what energies need to be moved around in the body!

Yoga, qigong and tai chi are all Eastern meditative practices specifically designed with the intention of moving energy through the body. Therefore, these are all fantastic opportunities to work with the chakra system. Local community and recreation centers and community colleges are great places to look for classes if you aren't familiar with any studios in your area that offer these modalities. The internet is a fantastic resource for finding classes near you. There are also many practitioners who offer online classes through various online streaming channels.

BODY LETTER 1

Instructions: Take some time and think about what you would like to tell your body. Start by taking a few deep breaths and just being silent. What messages do you want to relay to your body? Just let the pen do the work for this automatic writing exercise!

Dear Body,

ALLERGY TEST

Instructions: This exercise is designed to get you in touch with your body. Your body will tell you what it needs if you ask, and listen for the answer. You can test your body with any of these methods: applied kinesiology (muscle testing), a pendulum or using the "True North" method. Remember to use positive statements when testing (ex: I am allergic to soy vs. I am not allergic to soy). If the answer has a positive reaction, then you may have an allergy or sensitivity at this time.

<u>Muscle Testing:</u> There are many different types of muscle testing. Please watch this video for more information: https://www.youtube.com/watch?v=c9ikRMlI-jY

<u>Pendulum:</u> Any weighted object on a string that can act as a pendulum (ex: necklace). Steady the pendulum and start by testing how the pendulum works with your energy by using true statements (ex: my name is _____; I was born in _____, etc.). Watch the direction in which the pendulum swings, keep testing with questions you know the answer to until you feel comfortable in how the pendulum responds to you. You are now ready to test for your allergies, but remember to use positive statements while testing as to not confuse yourself!

<u>True North:</u> When facing North, your body naturally aligns with the Earth's magnetic field. To utilize this method, stand with your feet firmly on the ground, shoulder width apart, with a relaxed stance, facing North (you can use your phone's compass to verify). Start by using true statements to test how your body reacts while using your internal compass. You will find that your body naturally reacts and sway either front or back with each statement. When you have tested with enough positive statements to know what your internal compass is, you are ready to test for your allergies!

MAJOR 8

- Y N Cow's Milk
- Y N Egg
- Y N Peanuts
- Y N Tree Nuts
- Y N Fish
- Y N Shellfish
- Y N Wheat
- Y N Soy

MILK

- Y N Cow
- Y N Goat
- Y N Soy
- Y N Coconut
- Y N Hemp
- Y N Almond
- Y N Cashew
- Y N Rice

MEAT

- Y N Beef
- Y N Bison
- Y N Chicken
- Y N Duck
- Y N Goat
- Y N Lamb/Mutton
- Y N Ostrich
- Y N Pork
- Y N Quail
- Y N Turkey

SEAFOOD

- Y N Clams
- Y N Crab
- Y N Crawfish
- Y N Lobster
- Y N Mussels
- Y N Oysters
- Y N Prawns
- Y N Scallops
- Y N Shrimp

NUTS & SEEDS

- Y N Almond
- Y N Brazil Nut
- Y N Cashew
- Y N Chestnut
- Y N Cocoa
- Y N Coconut
- Y N Flaxseed
- Y N Hazelnut
- Y N Mustard Seed
- Y N Macadamia Nut
- Y N Pecan
- Y N Pine Nut
- Y N Pistachio
- Y N Poppy Seed
- Y N Praline
- Y N Pumpkin Seed
- Y N Sesame Seeds
- Y N Sunflower Seeds
- Y N Walnuts

GRAINS

Y N Amaranth*		Y N Rice* / Wild Rice*
Y N Barley		Y N Rye
Y N Buckwheat*		Y N Sorghum*
Y N Bulgur		Y N Spelt
Y N Corn*		Y N Teff*
Y N Farro		Y N Wheat
Y N Freekah		
Y N Millet*		*GLUTEN FREE
Y N Oats*		
Y N Quinoa*		

HERBS & SPICES

Y	N	Allspice	Y	N	Fennel	Y	N	Peppermint
Y	N	Anise	Y	N	Fenugreek	Y	N	Rosemary
Y	N	Basil	Y	N	Garlic	Y	N	Safflower
Y	N	Bay leaf	Y	N	Ginger	Y	N	Saffron
Y	N	Caper	Y	N	Horseradish	Y	N	Sage
Y	N	Cardamom	Y	N	Lavender	Y	N	Spearmint
Y	N	Caraway	Y	N	Lemon balm	Y	N	Star anise
Y	N	Chili pepper	Y	N	Lemongrass	Y	N	Sumac
Y	N	Chives	Y	N	Licorice	Y	N	Tarragon
Y	N	Cilantro	Y	N	Marjoram	Y	N	Thyme
Y	N	Cinnamon	Y	N	Mint	Y	N	Turmeric
Y	N	Clove	Y	N	Nutmeg	Y	N	Vanilla
Y	N	Coriander	Y	N	Oregano	Y	N	Wasabi
Y	N	Cumin	Y	N	Paprika	Y	N	**Wintergreen**
Y	N	Curry leaf	Y	N	Parsley			
Y	N	Dill	Y	N	Pepper - black			
Y	N	Elderflower	Y	N	Pepper – red			

VEGETABLES

Y	N	Artichoke	Y	N	Beet greens	Y	N	Okra
Y	N	Arugula	Y	N	Bok choy	Y	N	Leek
Y	N	Asparagus	Y	N	Broccoli	Y	N	Onion
Y	N	Eggplant	Y	N	Brussels sprouts	Y	N	Shallot
Y	N	Alfalfa sprouts	Y	N	Cabbage	Y	N	Scallion
Y	N	A(d)zuki beans	Y	N	Calabrese	Y	N	Radicchio
Y	N	Bean sprouts	Y	N	Carrots	Y	N	Rhubarb
Y	N	Black beans	Y	N	Cauliflower	Y	N	Radish
Y	N	Black-eyed peas	Y	N	Celery	Y	N	Spinach
Y	N	Chickpeas	Y	N	Chard	Y	N	Squash
Y	N	Green bean	Y	N	Collard greens	Y	N	Tomato
Y	N	Kidney beans	Y	N	Corn	Y	N	Potato
Y	N	Lentils	Y	N	Endive	Y	N	Sunchokes
Y	N	Lima/butter	Y	N	Fennel	Y	N	Sweet potato
Y	N	Mung beans	Y	N	Kale	Y	N	Taro
Y	N	Navy beans	Y	N	Kohlrabi	Y	N	Yam
Y	N	Pinto beans	Y	N	Lettuce	Y	N	Turnip greens
Y	N	Runner beans	Y	N	Mushrooms	Y	N	Water chestnut
Y	N	Split peas	Y	N	Mustard greens	Y	N	Watercress
Y	N	Peas	Y	N	Nettles	Y	N	**Zucchini**

FRUITS

Y	N	Apple	Y	N	Fig	Y	N	Melon
Y	N	Apricot	Y	N	Goji berry	Y	N	Cantaloupe
Y	N	Avocado	Y	N	Gooseberry	Y	N	Honeydew
Y	N	Banana	Y	N	Grape	Y	N	Watermelon
Y	N	Bilberry	Y	N	Raisin	Y	N	Miracle fruit
Y	N	Blackberry	Y	N	Grapefruit	Y	N	Mulberry
Y	N	Blackcurrant	Y	N	Guava	Y	N	Nectarine
Y	N	Blueberry	Y	N	Honeyberry	Y	N	Nance
Y	N	Boysenberry	Y	N	Huckleberry	Y	N	Olive
Y	N	Currant	Y	N	Jabuticaba	Y	N	Orange
Y	N	Cherry	Y	N	Jackfruit	Y	N	Blood orange
Y	N	Cherimoya	Y	N	Jambul	Y	N	Clementine
Y	N	Cloudberry	Y	N	Jujube	Y	N	Mandarine
Y	N	Coconut	Y	N	Juniper berry	Y	N	Tangerine
Y	N	Cranberry	Y	N	Kiwi	Y	N	Papaya
Y	N	Cucumber	Y	N	Kumquat	Y	N	Passionfruit
Y	N	Custard apple	Y	N	Lemon	Y	N	Peach
Y	N	Damson	Y	N	Lime	Y	N	Pear
Y	N	Date	Y	N	Loquat	Y	N	Persimmon
Y	N	Dragon fruit	Y	N	Longan	Y	N	Physalis
Y	N	Durian	Y	N	Lychee	Y	N	Plantain
Y	N	Elderberry	Y	N	Mango	Y	N	Plum
Y	N	Feijoa	Y	N	Marion berry	Y	N	Prune (dried plum)
Y	N	Pineapple	Y	N	Salmonberry	Y	N	Solanum quitoense
Y	N	Plumcot (or pluot)	Y	N	Rambutan	Y	N	Strawberry

Y	N	Pomegranate	Y	N	Redcurrant	Y	N	Tamarillo
Y	N	Pomelo	Y	N	Salal berry	Y	N	Tamarind
Y	N	Purple mangosteen	Y	N	Salak	Y	N	Ugli fruit
Y	N	Quince	Y	N	Satsuma	Y	N	Yuzu
Y	N	Raspberry	Y	N	Star fruit			

MINDFUL MEAL

Instructions: Take some time today to eat a mindful meal! What does that mean?

- Eat slowly – Take time to chew your food so that it is properly digested
- Savor the silence – Enjoy the time that you are eating and focus only on the sensation of eating.
- Zero electronics – Turn off your cell phone and television during your meal. Appreciate your surroundings without distraction today!
- Pay attention to the flavor – Engage all your senses and pay attention to the flavors, textures, smells, of what you are consuming
- Know your food – Do you know where your ingredients came from? Try and develop a connection not only to the food, but to the local, natural flavor.

What did you notice about your Mindful Meal?

_____
_____
_____
_____
_____

How did your Mindful Meal feel?

_____
_____
_____
_____
_____

Did your meal taste better than it normally does?

_____
_____
_____
_____
_____

WATCH A DOCUMENTARY

Instructions: Please take some extra time today to educate yourself on various food matters in our world. There are a number of great documentaries available on various streaming services.

Netflix:
- Fed Up
- Forks Over Knives
- Food, Inc.
- Hungry for Change
- Fat, Sick & Nearly Dead
- Far, Sick & Nearly Dead 2
- Vegucated
- Cowspiracy
- GMO OMG

Hulu:
- Hungry for Change
- Fat, Sick & Nearly Dead

Ted Talks:
- Why I'm a weekday vegetarian
- Teach every child about food
- What's wrong with what we eat
- The killer American diet that's sweeping the planet

What were your takeaways from the video you watched?

_____
_____
_____

How has your perspective on food changed?

_____
_____
_____

What will you implement now?

_____
_____
_____
_____

… RELEASE DENSITY & SHIFT YOUR LIFE

WEEK OF:

MY GOAL THIS WEEK IS:

I WILL ACCOMPLISH MY GOAL THIS WEEK BY TAKING THESE ACTIONS:
01.
02.
03.

HABIT	S	M	T	W	T	F	S
8+ GLASSES H2O							
5+ SERVINGS FRUIT & VEGGIES							
LEAN PROTEIN ONLY							
HOMEMADE FOOD ONLY							
NATURAL SUGARS ONLY							
ALCOHOL FREE							
SWEATY MOVEMENT							
MIND							
BODY							
SPIRIT							

Release Density & Shift Your Life!

WEEK FOUR
MIND BODY CONNECTION + GRATITUDE

Our thoughts, feelings, beliefs, and attitudes can positively or negatively impact our biological functioning. In other words, what is the story you are telling yourself? Since the word "mind" comes first in Mind, Body and Spirit, the mind must be in alignment before everything else can fall into place. You are creating your own reality by what you are expressing to yourself. Even if you have healthy physical habits, it's important to have a healthy inner dialogue. Your body is always listening, so what you tell yourself is critical. Improving the mind body connection can:

- improve the function of the immune system
- reduce pain
- lower blood pressure
- reduce damaging stress hormones
- reduce the need for some medications
- help prevent disease

There are a number of Mind Body Therapies that seek to create positive collaboration between the mind and the physical body including:

- Cognitive-behavioral therapy (CBT)
- Meditation
- Prayer
- Creative arts therapies (art, music, dance)
- Yoga
- Biofeedback

- Tai Chi
- Qi Gong
- Hypnosis
- Guided Imagery

The mind body connection is quite curious in that the body does not know the difference between what is real and what is imagined. The body only knows what the mind tells it. You will get to experience this phenomena during the Mental Vacation exercise this week. But for now, I want you to start thinking about how this concept affects our society. Right now, the entertainment industry is taking full advantage of this concept with the expansion of virtual reality systems into the mainstream markets. People can now turn their phones into virtual reality devices and be instantly transported into space, the ocean or even onto a roller coaster. The technology is fascinating and makes for a true to life experience, but makes me question the amount of what we let affect us without being fully aware. This is one of the reasons I am not a proponent of violence, especially in video games. Most video games are formatted as a role playing game (RPG) and are often set up to view in first person. In doing this, a deep sense authenticity is created for the game, however, knowing what we do about the mind body connection, viewing illicit behaviors from a first person perspective is where my concern lies. Couple that with the potential side effects and eventual desensitization of individuals, this makes for a scary future if left unexplored. What other situations can you think of that may be using the mind body connection?

So how can you learn to use the mind body connection to improve your life? If you haven't shifted the energy within you (your perspective, your attitude, your emotions), the Universe can't give you what you want because you wouldn't accept it. What exactly do I mean by that? If you are still telling yourself that you don't deserve a promotion, that you are no good at your job, and that you are worthless and should quit, there is no way that you would feel confident enough to accept a promotion, even if it was offered to you. So what is the story you are telling yourself? Are you worthy? Yes! Are you important? Yes! Are you needed here? YES!

Something that I often ask myself and my clients is "who's driving the car?" Are you in the drivers seat, making all of the critical choices in your life? Or are you in the backseat letting another take control of your path? Maybe you're letting your overprotective mother drive, telling you exactly what to do and when to do it, not realizing that you are an adult capable of making your own decisions. Or maybe your spouse is driving the car, putting your wants, needs and desires to the side. Maybe it's your children who have taken over the car and you aren't taking care of yourself. Your emotions could also be driving the car, fear is fast to take over and control where there is an element of self-doubt.

So what thoughts are motivating you? What do you choose to focus on? We take in over 4000 pieces of information per day, however our brains can only focus on 200 of them. Information gets thrown at us a mile a minute, some of it so basic that we don't even consider it "information" such as going outside and seeing that the sky is blue and the grass is green (okay, depending on where you live and what time of year it is, but you get the idea). There are many other types of information that we receive which are more subjective, such as expressions on people's faces, information from media (text on news print, sound and video on television, etc.) to anything that is coming through our phones. Anything that the brain has to interpret can be considered information, so with so much stimuli in our world, what are you choosing to focus on?

Gratitude is one of the most important methods of utilizing the mind body connection. It can boost happiness and reduces stress by:

- Savoring positive life experiences
- Improving self worth & self esteem
- Encouraging moral behavior
- Building social bonds, strengthening existing relationships & nurturing new ones
- Inhibiting comparisons
- Being incompatible with negative emotions
- Diminishing anger, bitterness, greed & curbing hedonic adaptation

ACTIVITIES:

- Body Letter 2 (92)
- Gratitude List (93)
- Random Act of Kindness (94)
- Mental Vacation (97)
- Gratitude Letter (98)
- Water, Consciousness & Intent (99)
- Epigenetics (100)

BODY LETTER 2

Instructions: Take some time and LISTEN to what you would like to tell your body. Start by taking a few deep breaths and just being silent. What messages does your body want to relay to you today? Just let the pen do the work for this automatic writing exercise!

Dear   ,

GRATITUDE LIST

FAMILY	HEALTH
1.	1.
2.	2.
3.	3.
4.	4.
5.	5.
CAREER	**SPIRITUALITY**
1.	1.
2.	2.
3.	3.
4.	4.
5.	5.
RELATIONSHIPS	**SELF DEVELOPMENT**
1.	1.
2.	2.
3.	3.
4.	4.
5.	5.

RELEASE DENSITY & SHIFT YOUR LIFE

RANDOM ACT OF KINDNESS

Instructions: Take some time today to do something for someone else and see how good you feel afterwards. Try to incorporate as many of these into your daily routine as possible as see how your life improves!

- Tweet or Facebook message a genuine compliment.
- Bring doughnuts (or a healthy treat, like cut-up fruit) to work.
- While you're out, compliment a parent on how well-behaved their child is.
- When everyone around you is gossiping about someone, be the one to butt in with something nice.
- Cook a meal or do a load of laundry for a friend who just had a baby or is going through a difficult time.
- If you walk by a car with an expired parking meter, put a quarter in it.
- Offer to take a photo of someone struggling to take a selfie - especially at a tourist location.
- Hang out with the person who just moved to town.
- Offer a homeless person your leftovers bag from the restaurant.
- Buy water and dog food for a homeless person you see with a dog
- Each time you get a new piece of clothing, donate an old one.
- Don't interrupt when someone else is speaking. (Surprisingly few people master this.)
- Email or write an old teacher who made a difference in your life.
- Compliment someone to their boss.
- Leave a nice server the biggest tip you can afford.
- Smile at someone on the street, just because.
- Let someone into your lane. They're probably in a rush just like you.
- Forgive someone, and never bring up the issue again.
- Talk to the shy person who's sitting by themselves at a party.
- Leave your newspaper or magazine behind for someone else to read at the coffee shop, the doctor's office, or on a plane.
- Help a mother with her baby stroller.
- Become a big brother or big sister.
- Let the person behind you at the supermarket checkout with one or two items go ahead of you.
- Write someone a letter. Like a real letter, on paper. And mail it!
- Give away stuff for free on Craigslist.
- Give someone a book you think they'd like.
- Be the person who puts a tip in the tip jar at the coffee shop. (Fewer people tip than you'd think!)
- Bring in fun office supplies to liven up the workday for everyone.
- When you go somewhere to get or do something, ask the people around you if you can pick up anything they need.
- Give someone a hug (if appropriate).
- If you notice spilled creamer or sugar on the counter at your coffee shop, wipe it up.
- Call your family. Call them!
- Donate your old eyeglasses so someone else can use them.
- When you're throwing something away on the street, pick up any litter around you and put that in the trash too.

- Write something nice on that person's updates who posts on Facebook constantly. They're probably lonely.
- Sincerely compliment your boss, who probably doesn't often get feedback from their reports.
- Put sticky notes with positive slogans on the mirrors in restrooms.
- Let them have the parking space.
- Relay an overheard compliment.
- Volunteer to read to kids at an after-school program.
- Bring your partner coffee in bed tomorrow.
- Try to make sure every person in a group conversation feels included.
- Answer that email you've been avoiding.
- Send anonymous flowers to the receptionist at work.
- Pay the toll for the person behind you.
- Donate or recycle your old laptop and electronics.
- Write a nice comment on your friend's blog.
- Play board games with senior citizens at a nursing home. (60% of them will never have a visitor during their stay)
- Give someone a tissue who's crying in the public, and offer to talk about it, but only if they want to.
- Listen intently.
- Adopt a rescue pet.
- Compliment someone in front of others.
- Hold the elevator.
- IM or email that person you're afraid to talk to because you don't want to "bother them." They're probably thinking the same thing about others!
- Remind yourself that everyone is fighting their own struggles.
- Leave some extra quarters in the laundry room or vending machine.
- Write your partner a list of things you love about them.
- Put together a small herb garden for someone.
- Empathize.
- Say thank you to a janitor.
- Talk to someone at work whom you haven't talked to before.
- Frame your friend's favorite lyric or quote and give it to them with a nice note.
- Send dessert to another table.
- Text someone just to say good morning or good night.
- Help your elderly neighbor take out the trash or mow their lawn.
- Give up your seat to someone (anyone!) on the bus or subway.
- Tell your siblings how much you appreciate them.
- Bring a security guard a hot cup of coffee.
- Plant a tree.
- Purchase some extra dog or cat food and drop it off at an animal shelter.
- If you're a good photographer, take photos of your friends and make them into a digital album.
- Send mail to a sick child.
- Wash someone's car.
- Offer to walk a neighbor's dog.
- Keep an extra umbrella at work and let someone borrow it on their way home if there's a sudden

downpour.
- Make two lunches and give one away.
- Reduce air pollution by carpooling.
- Say yes at the store when the cashier asks if you want to donate $1 to whichever cause.
- Be encouraging!
- Help someone struggling with heavy bags.
- Take all your change to the Coinstar machine and donate your collection to charity.
- Give your friend a hug, touch their arm, or pat them on the back. So many of us are starved for human touch!
- Buy lemonade from a kid's lemonade stand.
- Give your partner the benefit of the doubt.
- Be kind to the customer service rep on the phone. It's not their fault.
- Do the dishes even if it's your roommate's turn.
- Give someone the rest of your pack of gum.
- Clean someone's windshield.
- Make plans with that person you've been putting off seeing.
- Offer to return a shopping cart to the store for someone loading groceries in their car.
- Host a clean up party on the beach or at a park.

Which Random Act of Kindness did you choose? Why?
_____
_____
_____
_____

How did it go?
_____
_____
_____
_____

How did you feel afterwards?
_____
_____
_____
_____

What was your biggest takeaway from your Random Act of Kindness?
_____
_____
_____
_____

MENTAL VACATION

Instructions: The brain can't tell the difference between visualization and actual experience, so use this mental hack to take a mini vacation today! Try and give yourself at least 5 minutes by setting a timer on your phone. Start by envisioning yourself on your favorite vacation. For example, if you like the beach: feel the sand between your toes, the warmth of the sun on the tops of your feet, the smell of the salty air, the gentle sea breeze across your face and just breathe in deeply, etc. Feel into all of the details, trying to recall everything that you can!

Where did you choose to go? Why?

_____
_____
_____
_____
_____
_____

How did you feel before your mental vacation?

_____
_____
_____
_____
_____
_____

How did you feel after your mental vacation?

_____
_____
_____
_____
_____
_____

What was your biggest takeaway from this exercise?

_____
_____
_____
_____
_____
_____

GRATITUDE LETTER

Instructions: Is there someone who did or said something that absolutely changed your life? Were you able to thank them properly? Do they know what it meant to you? Maybe it was a stranger who did a kind act or shared a nice word, an old teacher who saw the light in you, or a boss who gave you an opportunity when no one else would. Take some time today to write them a letter of gratitude thanking them for what they did for you and how they changed your life. Don't feel like you have to share this letter with them if you don't want to or are unable to track them down, however if you feel comfortable enough and have the opportunity, it is always a beautiful gift to share with someone to let them know how they touched your life.

WATER, CONCIOUSNESS & INTENT

Instructions: Have you heard of Dr. Masaru Emoto and his groundbreaking studies on water? He studied how water reacts to different words, ideas and messages. Today, please watch this short video online (https://youtu.be/tAvzsjcBtx8) so you can start to familiarize yourself with his teachings and findings. If you have some more time, please feel free to watch the full documentary (approx. 30 minutes vs. the 3 minute option) also located online here (https://youtu.be/PDW9Lqj8hmc).

What did you learn from this video?

How do you think your thoughts are affecting you?

How can you use what you learned from this video to improve your life?

EPIGENETICS

Instructions: For this activity, you will read three different articles talking about the some of the newest research regarding the concept of DNA and how what our ancestors experienced can affect us today. Please read:

- Trauma Has Genetic Impact For Native Americans | Care2 Causes - http://bit.ly/2nNUQaw
- Study of Holocaust survivors finds trauma passed on to children's genes | Science | The Guardian - http://bit.ly/2mYjeZs
- Post-Traumatic Slave Syndrome and Intergenerational Trauma: Slavery is Like a Curse Passing Through the DNA of Black People - Atlanta Black Star - http://bit.ly/2nOj8Bi

What did you learn from these articles?

What came up for you as you read these articles?

Can you identify any situations within your own family history similar to this?

RELEASE DENSITY & SHIFT YOUR LIFE

WEEK OF:

MY GOAL THIS WEEK IS:

I WILL ACCOMPLISH MY GOAL THIS WEEK BY TAKING THESE ACTIONS:
01.

02.

03.

HABIT	S	M	T	W	T	F	S
8+ GLASSES H2O							
5+ SERVINGS FRUIT & VEGGIES							
LEAN PROTEIN ONLY							
HOMEMADE FOOD ONLY							
NATURAL SUGARS ONLY							
ALCOHOL FREE							
SWEATY MOVEMENT							
MIND							
BODY							
SPIRIT							

Release Density & Shift Your Life!

WEEK FIVE
FORGIVENESS

This is one of those very tricky topics to write in depth about. I go into much more detail in the online group depending on the needs of the class, but I do want to share a few thoughts surrounding the idea:

- Forgiveness doesn't mean you excuse the crime, it just means you're no longer willing to be a victim.
- When we blame others we hand over our authority instead of taking responsibility.
- As with any difficult situation, what was the deeper value gained? The silver lining? The lesson earned?
- When there is guilt, there is often underlying blame. Guilt is often anger turned inward.
- If it were meant to be different, it would have been.
- Sometimes "role models" are models of what we *don't* want to be.
- Procrastination is a fear based pattern. Fear of not doing well, not being accepted, lack of self-love.
- At the bottom of every fear (unnatural fear) is almost always struggle with self worth and self esteem.

Self esteem	**Self worth**
Your perception of your value	Your innate value
The way you see your value	What your value truly is

Your perception of your value and your innate value are meant to be in alignment - they should be the same. We compare and observe reactions of people around us to our actions, as we take responsibility for others emotions, feelings, actions, based on other people react to us or not (starts with family typically), we feel that we must have the acceptance of others to feel that we are good enough, instead of looking inwards to find that self love and self acceptance. As you are going through this week's activities, I invite you to be extra kind and loving with yourself and really honor the self care that your body needs and craves.

ACTIVITIES:

- Body List & Flip (110)
- Forgiveness – Others (111)
- Forgiveness – Self (112)
- Self Esteem (113)
- Self Worth (114)
- Bring Energy Back (115)
- Timeline (116)

BODY LIST & FLIP

Instructions: What don't you like about your body? List 10 things that you don't like about your body. Then you are going to shift each statement to a positive statement.

EX: I don't like how much I sweat. FLIPPED TO: My body knows how to properly purge itself of toxins.

1. Flip to:
2. Flip to:
3. Flip to:
4. Flip to:
5. Flip to:
6. Flip to:
7. Flip to:
8. Flip to:
9. Flip to:
10. Flip to:

FORGIVENESS – OTHERS

Instructions: What area in your life needs forgiveness? Lets focus on other people, situations or specific experiences. Start with three. Ask yourself: How can I shift my vibration around that to a point of awareness, growth insight and value? Find the value in that experience.

I forgive…

I forgive…

I forgive…

FORGIVENESS – SELF

Instructions: What area in your life needs forgiveness? Lets focus on yourself, situations or specific experiences. Start with three. Ask yourself: How can I shift my vibration around that to a point of awareness, growth insight and value? Find the value in that experience.

I forgive…

I forgive…

I forgive…

SELF ESTEEM

What is your definition of self esteem?

_____

How does your self esteem affect you?

_____

What is more important – how others value you or how YOU value you?

_____

SELF WORTH

What is your definition of self worth?

_____

How does your self worth affect you?

_____

Where did your ideas of self worth come from?

_____

BRING ENERGY BACK

Instructions: Let's spend some time today taking back energy that you've given to anyone else - things that haunt, irritate or still bother you. For this exercise, visualize a person in your mind's eye and see them as different colors. Ask yourself "is there any of my color still in them?" If so, take your energy back with gratitude, love and appreciation. Repeat as many times as is necessary, for as many people as is necessary.

How did this exercise feel?

___

How many people did you take back energy from?

___

How do you feel after bringing your energy back?

___

TIME LINE

Instructions: Take some time today to think about your own life. You will fill in a time line of all of the situations that you want forgiveness for, whether it is for yourself or for other people. I would like you to do this on a separate sheet of paper outside of this book. When you have filled in a timeline and you don't think that you have any more situations you are ready to release, I would like you to burn the piece of paper. Burning this paper will serve as a form of energetic release that you will be able to feel on a physical and emotional level.

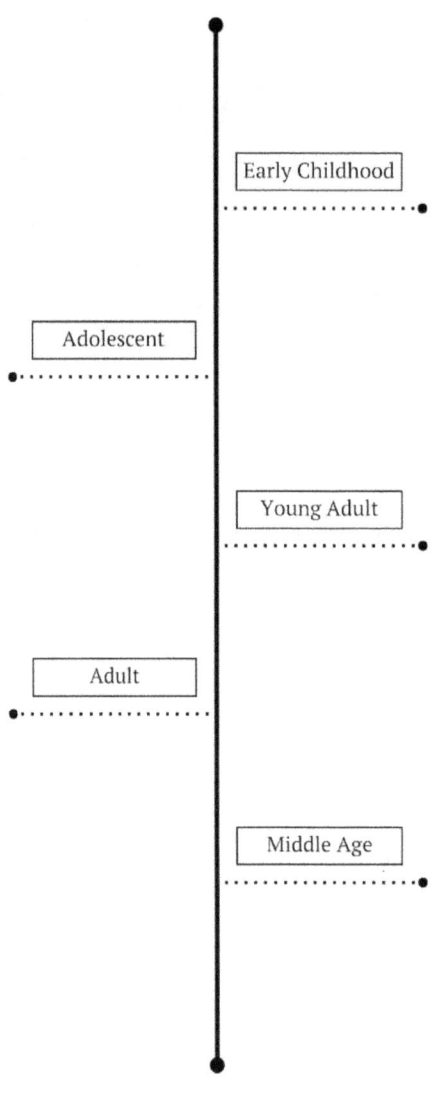

RELEASE DENSITY & SHIFT YOUR LIFE

WEEK OF:

MY GOAL THIS WEEK IS:

I WILL ACCOMPLISH MY GOAL THIS WEEK BY TAKING THESE ACTIONS:
01.
02.
03.

HABIT	S	M	T	W	T	F	S
8+ GLASSES H2O							
5+ SERVINGS FRUIT & VEGGIES							
LEAN PROTEIN ONLY							
HOMEMADE FOOD ONLY							
NATURAL SUGARS ONLY							
ALCOHOL FREE							
SWEATY MOVEMENT							
MIND							
BODY							
SPIRIT							

Release Density & Shift Your Life!

WEEK SIX
LOVE + BOUNDARIES

Setting boundaries is a way of loving and caring for yourself. Personal boundaries are where you decide what types of communication, behavior, and interaction are acceptable to you. Setting and keeping boundaries is about honoring your feelings, defining where you end and others begin, both psychically and emotionally. When you don't assert healthy boundaries you are essentially giving up your right to choose and your power.

If you never learned how to establish healthy boundaries trying to figure out how to set them can be challenging. If your boundaries are too lax you end up allowing other people's boundaries to dictate what happens to you. On the other hand having overly rigid boundaries creates it's own set of problems with intolerance and control. No matter where you fall on the boundary spectrum, awareness is the first step to establishing, changing and enforcing healthy boundaries.

Without a strong sense of boundary to our emotional body, we take on emotional pollutants and toxins from other people and places. We lose boundaries, sometimes we make connections to others and such connections create an inappropriate flow of energy. We take energy from others or let others take our energy, creating harmful psychic cords. We are linked through our emotional body, and through various chakras. When someone can "pull your strings" they are literally pulling your energy.

Let's start by checking into your boundaries:
- Do you say yes when you really want to say no?
- Do you apologize often?
- Do you avoid confrontation?
- Do you put everyone else's needs above your own?

I want to discuss the idea of **protect vs. maintain**. Frequently in the world of healing you will hear people discussing the idea of needing to "protect" themselves from other people, or other entities whom they feel may have bad or negative energy. I really hate the idea of needing to protect yourself, just the word protect indicates that we are less than and in a space of being threatened. If we reframe it and we talk about our energy in terms of maintaining it, we have the understanding that we are holding our own space and are not threatened by external sources. This goes along with the concept I talk a lot about: being **proactive vs. reactive.** Are you only worrying about your energy and maintaining boundaries after something has happened and you're already upset, or are you taking action every single day to maintain your energy so you are not phased by certain behaviors?

ACTIVITIES:

- Love Letter (125)
- Role Models (126)
- 5 Love Languages (127)
- Vulnerability (128)
- Self Love List (129)
- Personal Mission Statement (130)
- Roles + Relationships (131)

LOVE LETTER

Instructions: Take a few minutes to center yourself before today's activity. Close your eyes and take three deep breaths in and out. Write a letter to yourself, not just any letter, a love letter. Try not to put too much thought into this activity. Put the pen to paper, and try some automatic writing. There is no wrong way to do it, except if you don't try!

ROLE MODELS

Instructions: What role models did you have in your life that taught your healthy thinking, boundaries and behaviors? If you didn't have role models that taught you healthy ones, what did your role models teach you? These may not always be your parents! Start with three.

5 LOVE LANGUAGES

Instructions: Please complete Gary Chapman's 5 Love Languages Quiz here (http://www.5lovelanguages.com). Have your partner and children do the same.

What were your love languages?
1.
2.
3.
4.
5.

What you surprised to find out your love language(s)?

_____
_____
_____
_____
_____
_____
_____
_____
_____

How about your partner or child's?

_____
_____
_____
_____
_____
_____
_____
_____
_____

How has your understanding of your partner or child changed since gaining a deeper understanding of your own needs?

_____
_____
_____
_____
_____
_____
_____
_____
_____

VULNERABILITY

Introductions: Please watch this TED Talk by Brene Brown on the topic of vulnerability here (http://www.ted.com/talks/brene_brown_on_vulnerability)

What were your takeaways from the video?
_____
_____
_____
_____
_____
_____
_____
_____
_____
_____
_____
_____

How do you feel about vulnerability?
_____
_____
_____
_____
_____
_____
_____
_____
_____
_____
_____
_____

How can you be more vulnerable?
_____
_____
_____
_____
_____
_____
_____
_____
_____
_____
_____
_____

SELF LOVE LIST

Instructions: Take some time today to think about some things that you really love about yourself. Please list ten of them below!

1. I LOVE…

2. I LOVE…

3. I LOVE…

4. I LOVE…

5. I LOVE…

6. I LOVE…

7. I LOVE…

8. I LOVE…

9. I LOVE…

10. I LOVE…

PERSONAL MISSION STATEMENT

Instructions: Create a personal mission statement, philosophy of life or creed. It focuses on what you want to be (character) and to do (contributions and achievements) and on the values and principles upon which being and doing are based. Once you have a clear mission to your life, it is easier to set and maintain boundaries that help to keep you on this path.

EX: To cultivate a universal responsibility for one another and the planet we share ~ The Dalai Lama

RELEASE DENSITY & SHIFT YOUR LIFE

ROLES + RELATIONSHIPS

Instructions: Boundaries are put in place for the various types of relationships that you have in your life. Think about list of different roles and relationships in which you are involved. Try to focus on people you have regular contact with. Write down your list in the space provided below.

\+ relationships you have most control over

Or

– relationships you have least control over.

1. Name:

What type of relationship is this?

_____
_____
_____

Who initiates contact?

_____
_____
_____

What is the time frame for this relationship?

_____
_____
_____

Is sharing equal in this relationship?

_____
_____
_____

Are there things that you would like to say in this relationship, but you do not or feel that you cannot? What are they?

_____
_____
_____

Do you feel that your own boundaries are respected in this relationship? Why or why not?

_____
_____
_____

What changes might you like to make in this relationship?

_____
_____
_____

2. Name:

What type of relationship is this?

Who initiates contact?

What is the time frame for this relationship?

Is sharing equal in this relationship?

Are there things that you would like to say in this relationship, but you do not or feel that you cannot? What are they?

Do you feel that your own boundaries are respected in this relationship? Why or why not?

What changes might you like to make in this relationship?

3. Name:

What type of relationship is this?

_____
_____
_____

Who initiates contact?

_____
_____
_____

What is the time frame for this relationship?

_____
_____
_____

Is sharing equal in this relationship?

_____
_____
_____

Are there things that you would like to say in this relationship, but you do not or feel that you cannot? What are they?

_____
_____
_____

Do you feel that your own boundaries are respected in this relationship? Why or why not?

_____
_____
_____

What changes might you like to make in this relationship?

_____
_____
_____

4. Name:

What type of relationship is this?

___

Who initiates contact?

___

What is the time frame for this relationship?

___

Is sharing equal in this relationship?

___

Are there things that you would like to say in this relationship, but you do not or feel that you cannot? What are they?

___

Do you feel that your own boundaries are respected in this relationship? Why or why not?

___

What changes might you like to make in this relationship?

___

5. Name:

What type of relationship is this?

Who initiates contact?

What is the time frame for this relationship?

Is sharing equal in this relationship?

Are there things that you would like to say in this relationship, but you do not or feel that you cannot? What are they?

Do you feel that your own boundaries are respected in this relationship? Why or why not?

What changes might you like to make in this relationship?

RELEASE DENSITY & SHIFT YOUR LIFE

RELEASE DENSITY & SHIFT YOUR LIFE

WEEK OF:

MY GOAL THIS WEEK IS:

I WILL ACCOMPLISH MY GOAL THIS WEEK BY TAKING THESE ACTIONS:
01.

02.

03.

HABIT	S	M	T	W	T	F	S
8+ GLASSES H2O							
5+ SERVINGS FRUIT & VEGGIES							
LEAN PROTEIN ONLY							
HOMEMADE FOOD ONLY							
NATURAL SUGARS ONLY							
ALCOHOL FREE							
SWEATY MOVEMENT							
MIND							
BODY							
SPIRIT							

Release Density & Shift Your Life!

WEEK SEVEN
HAPPINESS + MOTIVATION

Did you know for every 100 articles in psychology on sadness or depression there is ONE on happiness? Why are we as a society not more focused on what makes us happy? Happiness is almost portrayed as a myth; something everyone wants, yet there is no prescribed method on how to get it. It is truly subjective and without reason at times, and one of the most sought after treasures of human kind. The idea that there should be a pursuit of happiness, however, is a sham. A pursuit would indicate that there is an end goal, yet happiness cannot be found. Every single day happiness is something to be cultivated and nurtured and then will flourish, but it is not something that is simply achieved one day and forgotten about the very next.

But what happens if you get something you've always dreamed of? Maybe you won the lottery, or came into some large amount of money, that would change everything, right? Wrong. The happiness bounce of external circumstance lasts around two years. So winning the lottery will not permanently give you all the happiness you think it will! High and rising expectations factor into this greatly, as people get used to the external circumstances due to hedonic adaptation. So what can do you to get around hedonic adaptation? Savor your experiences by:

- Appreciating
- Story-telling
- Scrap-booking
- Celebrating
- Complimenting
- Living mindfully
- Going through bitter-sweet nostalgia

Well if winning the lottery can't make you happy, what can? You. You are in control of how you choose to approach each and every day. It is important to note however that some happiness is not within your control. In her book, *The How of Happiness: A Scientific Approach to Getting the Life You Want* author Sonja Lyubomirsky explains that 50% of your happiness is genetically related, 10% is circumstantial and 40% is up to you. Meaning that you do inherit certain things from your parents and ancestors in regards to your level of happiness (remember reading up on epigenetics?), but it's not all about the genetics, that's only half the story. The circumstantial 10% is like what we were talking about – winning the lottery, or whatever set of circumstances you think is or will greatly impact your life, like that brand new sports car. The most important part is that 40% of your happiness is up to you – how you choose to spend you time, effort and energy doing what does (or conversely, doesn't) make you happy. The happiest people in the world have these things in common:

- Spending time with friends and family
- Optimism
- Gratitude
- Lending a helping hand
- Savoring pleasures
- Regular exercise
- Pursuing lifelong goals
- Strength, coping and resilience in times of trouble
- Strong sense of community

Sometimes it can be hard to find happiness, or stay happy when we are unmotivated or unsure of where our motivation lies. Motivation, like happiness, is a muscle and can be developed over time with patience and practice! Here are some things you can do to increase your motivation:

- Set small, measurable goals
- Develop a personal mantra
- Commit publicly
- Create your own routine and rituals
- Keep up the optimism
- Visualize your goals
- Face your fears
- Power pose to increase confidence
- Personal Pep talk
- Get present!

Optimists view good things as due to SOMETHING GOOD INSIDE and that good things will last a LONG time, while pessimists view good things as due to LUCK and believe that they will last a SHORT time. [the vice versa also true]. So what can you do to be purposefully become more optimistic?

- Keep a diary of goals
- Join a group where you feel encouraged or encourage others
- Identify barrier thoughts and replace with other options
- Rubber band bracelet – Wear a rubber band around your wrist and every time you identify a negative thought, snap the band onto your skin. The body will start to identify the snap of the band with the negative thought which will curb the negativity.
- Make optimism a habit!

ACTIVITIES:

- Self Sabotage (146)
- Authentic Happiness Inventory (147)
- The Hidden Power of Smiling (148)
- What makes a good life? (149)
- Best Possible Self (150)
- Motivation Deep Dive (151)
- Watch a Documentary (152)

ARIELLE STERLING

SELF SABOTAGE

Instructions: Do you notice that you are stuck in self-sabotaging habits? Pick ten areas that you want to shift for yourself. Create an affirmation for each area of self-sabotage.

EX: I wait until the last minute to complete tasks. SHIFT TO: I give myself appropriate time to complete my tasks.

1.
Shift to:

2.
Shift to:

3.
Shift to:

4.
Shift to:

5.
Shift to:

6.
Shift to:

7.
Shift to:

8.
Shift to:

9.
Shift to:

10.
Shift to:

AUTHENTIC HAPPINESS INVENTORY

Instructions: Please revisit the Authentic Happiness Inventory that you took during Week One. Take the self assessment online again and let's check into where you are at.

How did your answers change from the first time you took this self assessment?

_____
_____
_____
_____
_____
_____
_____
_____
_____
_____
_____
_____

What did you learn about yourself?

_____
_____
_____
_____
_____
_____
_____
_____
_____
_____
_____
_____

What changes will you keep making to continue to improve your happiness rating?

_____
_____
_____
_____
_____
_____
_____
_____
_____
_____
_____
_____

THE HIDDEN POWER OF SMILING

Instructions: Please watch this TED Talk on The Hidden Power of Smiling and answer the following questions below. You can find the video here (http://www.ted.com/talks/ron_gutman_the_hidden_power_of_smiling?language=en)

What did you learn about smiling?

What else did you take away from this video?

How will you smile more?

RELEASE DENSITY & SHIFT YOUR LIFE

WHAT MAKES A GOOD LIFE?

Instructions: Please watch this TED Talk on What Makes a Good Life and answer the following questions below. You can find the video here (https://ed.ted.com/featured/zt8LPHB1)

What makes a good life?

What else did you take away from this video?

How will you apply what you learned?

BEST POSSIBLE SELF

Instructions: Take a few minutes to visualize your best possible self. Imagine your life in vivid details think of yourself as reaching your potential, hitting an important milestone, or realizing one of your life dreams. After you have a fairly clear image, write about the details. Be sure to write about the strength of character that you observe in your vision. Also, write about what character strengths will you need to deploy to make this best possible self a reality!

MOTIVATION DEEP DIVE

What is your driving factor each and every day?

_____
_____
_____
_____
_____
_____
_____
_____
_____
_____
_____

Why does this motivate you?

_____
_____
_____
_____
_____
_____
_____
_____
_____
_____
_____

For whom are you doing this work?

_____
_____
_____
_____
_____
_____
_____
_____
_____
_____
_____

WATCH A DOCUMENTARY

Please take some extra time today to watch a documentary on Happiness. There are a number of great documentaries available on various streaming services.

Netflix:
- Happy
- Happy People
- Minimalism
- The Kindness Diaries

Ted Talks:
- The Surprising Science of Happiness
- Choice, happiness and spaghetti sauce
- Happiness and its surprises
- Flow, the secret to happiness
- Want to be happy? Be grateful
- Remember to say thank you

What were your takeaways from the video you watched?

_____
_____
_____

How has your perspective on happiness changed?

_____
_____
_____

What will you implement now?

_____
_____
_____
_____

RELEASE DENSITY & SHIFT YOUR LIFE

WEEK OF:

MY GOAL THIS WEEK IS:

I WILL ACCOMPLISH MY GOAL THIS WEEK BY TAKING THESE ACTIONS:
01.

02.

03.

HABIT	S	M	T	W	T	F	S
8+ GLASSES H2O							
5+ SERVINGS FRUIT & VEGGIES							
LEAN PROTEIN ONLY							
HOMEMADE FOOD ONLY							
NATURAL SUGARS ONLY							
ALCOHOL FREE							
SWEATY MOVEMENT							
MIND							
BODY							
SPIRIT							

Release Density & Shift Your Life!

WEEK EIGHT
MAGIC + MANIFESTATION

What is magic? Per the definition of Merriam Webster, magic is:

1 a : the use of means (as charms or spells) believed to have supernatural power over natural forces

  b : magic rites or incantations

2 a : an extraordinary power or influence seemingly from a supernatural source

  b : something that seems to cast a spell : enchantment

3 : the art of producing illusions by sleight of hand entertained with acts of jugglery and magic

I think that leaves it really open for interpretation as to what you consider to be magic. Look through the eyes of children, they see the world in a much more pure and joyful vantage point. How do you define extraordinary? From there you can determine what is magic in your life! Is it thinking about someone and having them call or text you? Is it thinking of an object and seeing it later on that day where your appointment is? Is it getting a free coffee because the person ahead of you paid it forward when you were having a shitty day and just wanted someone to cut you a break? It's all up to you what you choose to see as magic in this world! Magic looks and feels different for each of us, but may be known by other words and experiences such as miracles, synchronicities or coincidences.

Manifestation goes along with being open to magic. What are you willing to bring in to your life? Here are some tips that I have found that are helpful in working to manifest and create magic in every day life:

- Small steps! By making a 1% positive shift every day, you know that you are moving forward!
- Feelings of self-doubt, guilt and shame don't have to be part of your internal world if you don't want to let them!
- Figure out who you really are and what you really want! This ensures you know what you really want to manifest and that you're manifesting for the right reasons!

- People who have never made mistakes have rarely ever achieved very much either. Your so-called "mistakes" are really valuable learning experiences that are setting your path..
- Trying to manifest too many things at once will scatter your energy. Focus in on what really matters, and pursue it with all your heart.
- Expect it to happen, **and it will.**
- Free yourself from caring about those who try to bring you down. Their judgments are about their own anxieties and failings—not yours.
- Act like you already have everything you want, and notice how much more quickly the things you wanted begin to appear in your life.
- When you change your attitude, the world changes around you to match your expectations and emotions.
- Be good to others every day, and watch how that goodness comes back to you.
- Your happiness is yours! Consider your accomplishments, your blessings, and choose to be happy.
- Live your way, not the way that friends, partners, colleagues or your parents told you that you must.
- If your goals or dreams don't fill you with an exciting charge, they're not the right ones. Look for intentions that are energized like a battery, and work towards manifesting those.

ACTIVITIES:

- Abundance Check (161)
- Vision Board (162)
- Placemat Exercise (163)
- Mind Mapping (164)
- The Secret (165)
- Ted Talk (166)
- 12 Universal Laws (167)

ABUNDANCE CHECK

```
YOUR HIGHER SELF                          DATE: _____
444 MANIFEST DESTINY WAY
PARADISE CITY, USA

PAY TO THE
ORDER OF: _____  $ [        ]
          _____ Dollars

                          BANK
                         OF THE
                         UNIVERSE
FOR: _____    SIGNED: _____
```

Instructions: This is a practical exercise in intention. When you write these checks, you are aligning your intention with the universe, signaling that you are ready and willing to receive. You can do this every month (up to 24 hours after the New Moon) to simply re-affirms that intention. Abundance checks are a tool we can use to create more abundance in our lives. It is not always financial, but certainly in an area that you need.

If you do not have a checking account you can draw a check on a piece of paper and fill it out the same way -- the results will be the same, more abundance for you. Here's how to do them:

1. Take a check from your check book. Where it says "Pay to," write your name.
2. In the little box on the same line where you would fill in a dollar amount write "Paid in full."
3. On the line underneath your name, where you would write out a dollar amount, write "Paid in full."
4. Sign the check: "The Law of Abundance."

Do not put a date on the check. Do not write a specific dollar amount in the check. Put in a safe place and forget about it. The Universe will take it from there!

VISION BOARD

Instructions: Once you determine what it is want in your life, you can create a vision board to help manifest it! By setting the intention that whatever you place on your board will come into being, you are creating power within yourself! This activity can be done any time of year, not just at the New Year! Your board can be as simple or as detailed as you'd like, but it should represent YOU and what you want. You can take photos from magazines to create a collage, or you can print off photos online – whatever feels best for you! There are even websites like Pinterest that allow you to create digital vision boards to collect thoughts and ideas. While I do utilize both, I would like you to create a tangible one today that you can post somewhere that you will see every day, whether it is in your office, at your desk, or on your bathroom mirror, it is important that you see it regularly!

How did you feel creating a vision board?

Were you surprised at what you were drawn to?

PLACEMAT EXERCISE

Instructions: This exercise is Abraham Hick's Placemat Exercise. On the left side of the page, write the things you really want to be, do or have today. Do not include things you have to do, should do or don't want to do. This is *not* your to do list for the day. This is an exercise to settle your mind on items that please you, that you are looking forward to, that inspire you. On the right side of the page, write the things you want the Universe to do or bring you today. This includes things over which you have no control, things you don't want to do but have to, or things you just don't want to think about. Whatever you would like the Universe to do, including bringing you certain states of being like joy, ask and it is given. Once you have completed your list, spend at least 17 seconds feeling pure positive emotion focusing on each item to manifest it into reality. Feel what it would feel like to have those items on the Universe's side of the page completed. Imagine having those things already done.

Things I Want to Be, Do or Have Today	Things I Want the Universe to Bring Me Today

MIND MAPPING

Instructions: This exercise is designed to get your brain moving, thinking and connecting in new ways. You will start with an idea at the center of the map and from there, map out other related ideas that come to mind as you start writing. There is no wrong way to do this exercise, other than to not do it!

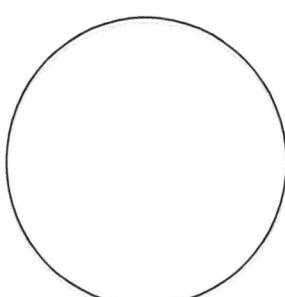

THE SECRET

Instructions: Please watch the documentary "The Secret". This can be found on streaming platforms Netflix and Hulu. If you do not have either of those streaming services, please check with your local library for the DVD copy. This documentary is well worth watching again even if you have seen it before, as some messages may resonate differently for you this time around. Consider having some friends over to watch this documentary together!

What were your takeaways from The Secret? If you had seen it before, how was it different now?

_____

_____

_____

_____

_____

_____

_____

_____

_____

What did you learn about the Law of Attraction?

_____

_____

_____

_____

_____

_____

_____

_____

What will you implement in your life now?

_____

_____

_____

_____

_____

_____

_____

TED TALKS: Magic

Instructions: Please take some extra time today to watch at least one of the following videos on magic from TED Talks:
- Helder Guimarães: A magical search for a coincidence
- Arthur Benjamin: The magic of Fibonacci numbers
- Keith Barry: Brain magic
- Eric Mead: The magic of the placebo
- Beau Lotto: Optical illusions show how we see
- Al Seckel: Visual illusions that show how we (mis)think

What were your takeaways from the video you watched?

How has your perspective on magic changed?

What will you implement now?

12 UNIVERSAL LAWS

Instructions: Please watch this video on the 12 Universal Laws (https://www.youtube.com/watch?v=7PIUuej-2EQ). If you already watched The Secret, you are familiar with the Law of Attraction, the remainder of Universal Laws are briefly covered in the video.

What were your takeaways from the video you watched?

_____
_____
_____
_____
_____
_____

How has your perspective on Universal Laws changed?

_____
_____
_____
_____
_____
_____

What will you implement now?

_____
_____
_____
_____
_____
_____
_____

RELEASE DENSITY & SHIFT YOUR LIFE

ABOUT THE AUTHOR

    Arielle Sterling is a Life Coach and Reiki Master. From a young age, Arielle knew she was different, having been keenly aware of her clairvoyant and clairaudient abilities and using them to help facilitate intuitive healing well over a decade before she acquired any formal training. Her empathic and psychic abilities became overwhelming and intense, eventually asking for her gifts to go away until the point in time that she could understand and utilize them with grace and ease as a young adult.

    Arielle received her first Reiki attunement in 2004 and has immersed herself in mastering holistic therapies since. She has studied a multitude of energy therapies including: Usui Reiki, Therapeutic Touch, Matrix Healing Technique: Electromagnetic Field & Body Integration, Lightbody Connection & Activation, DNA Cell(f) Imagery & Communication, and Spiritual Surgery. Arielle has studied with world-renowned psychic mediums, intuitive healers, angel communicators and astrologists to advance her own psychic and mediumship gifts. Her wide variety of modalities provides for a unique healing experience for every client.

    For more information or to book a session, please visit www.ariellesterling.com.

www.ingramcontent.com/pod-product-compliance
Lightning Source LLC
Chambersburg PA
CBHW081216230426
43666CB00015B/2760